Free Speech

RESOURCE BOOK

Bettman/Corbis

ABC-CLIO

PROJECT EDITOR
Holly Heinzer, *Project Editor*

EDITORIAL
Lynn Jurgensen, *Managing Editor*
David Tipton, *Managing Editor*
Kirk Werner, *Managing Editor*
Liza Hickey, *Editor*
Pat Carlin, *Senior Editor*
Elisabeth McCaffery, *Writer/Editor*
Allen Raichelle, *Senior Editor*
Tim O'Donnell, *Consulting Editor*
Melissa Stallings, *Consulting Editor*

MEDIA ACQUISITIONS
Caroline Price, *Manager, Media Resources*

PRODUCTION EDITOR
Vicki Moran, *Senior Production Editor*

Ann Claunch, *Director of Curriculum*

National History Day, Inc.

DESIGNERS
The Winter Group

Library of Congress Cataloging-in-Publication Data
Free speech : resource book.
     p. cm. -- (Triumph & tragedy in history)
   Includes bibliographical references and index.
   ISBN 1-59884-014-2 (workbook : alk. paper)
   1. Freedom of speech--Study and teaching--Activity programs.
  2. Freedom of speech--United States.   I. Series.
JC591.F774 2006
323.44'30973--dc22

2006014912

COVER PHOTO: Gregory Lee Johnson, defendant in flag burning case, speaking against constitutional amendment banning flag desecration, outside Capitol.
Photo by Cynthia Johnson/Time Life Pictures/Getty Images

Contents

Corbis

Time Life Pictures/Getty Images

About the Development Team

ABC-CLIO AND NATIONAL HISTORY DAY are proud to partner together to bring you the *Triumph & Tragedy* Series. We are grateful to the team that developed the series, especially Charles Mullin, Chris Mullin, and Brett Piersma who wrote the scholarly context and classroom activities to engage students in the process of historical inquiry. In addition, we want to thank the staff members from both organizations who provided background content and resources. A special thank you to Holly Heinzer, Caroline Price, and Vicki Moran who spent countless hours in leading the team through the development process.

CHARLES MULLIN
UNIVERSITY OF CALIFORNIA SANTA BARBARA
Charles Mullin received his B.A. in Communication Studies from UCLA and his M.A. and Ph.D. in Communication from UC Santa Barbara. In addition to his interest in First Amendment law and the analysis of free speech issues, his scholarly pursuits include the societal- and individual-level effects of the mass media, and the laws and policies that impact the media universe. His research has included studies on such diverse topics as the relationship between media exposure and attitudes toward the law, the effects of pretrial publicity on juror decision making, the effects of sexually violent films on attitudes toward victims of domestic violence, and more recently, the network of attitudes and behaviors associated with Internet sharing of music files. He is currently on the faculty of the Communication Department at UC Santa Barbara, where he teaches a variety of courses pertaining in some way to the relationship between the media, the law, and society.

CHRIS MULLIN
SANTA YNEZ VALLEY UNION HIGH SCHOOL
Chris Mullin graduated from the University of California at Berkeley with a degree in Classical Greek and Latin and received his Masters in Education from the University of California at Santa Barbara. Chris teaches Latin, AP European History, and AP United States History in the beautiful Santa Ynez Valley, California at Santa Ynez Valley Union High School. Chris has been a

fellow of the Teachers Network Leadership Institute, Facilitator for the California History-Social Science Project, and has developed numerous history-related classroom activities that he has presented at state and national conferences. In 2003, Chris was named California Teacher of the Year for his passionate and innovative approaches to teaching history. Chris is dedicated to finding innovative ways to introduce primary source materials into the day-to-day teaching of history. He believes in challenging students and encouraging them to see history not as a series of verifiable facts, but rather as a compendium of open-ended questions. In lectures, he makes a point of revealing his own reflective process, in order to help students hone their own critical thinking skills.

BRETT PIERSMA
SANTA YNEZ VALLEY UNION HIGH SCHOOL

Brett Piersma received his B.A. in History and his Masters of Education and teaching credential at the University of California at Santa Barbara. He teaches AP European History, AP American Government, and College Preparatory World Cultures at Santa Ynez Valley Union High School in Santa Ynez, California. He has facilitated the California History-Social Sciences Project at UCSB and is a MetLife Fellow for the Teachers Network Leadership Institute. Brett has also co-written several award-winning classroom activities. His many passions in teaching include designing primary source-based lesson plans, increasing teacher voice and leadership in schools, increasing student access to rigorous curricula, and perfecting the use of technology in the classroom. Among his innovative techniques are dress-up nights for AP European History students that recreate an Enlightenment-era *salon,* complete with period music and debates on the works of Voltaire and Rousseau.

Foreword

The *Triumph & Tragedy* series explores three issues currently central to American public discourse: free speech, immigration, and nation-building. None of these topics has arisen overnight; in fact, they have been with us for centuries. This is because all three go to the heart of the American experience and our national aspirations: we are a nation of immigrants who dedicated our country to freedom and liberty, within our borders and across the world. Our treatment of our civil liberties, our new arrivals, and our responsibility to other nations defines who we are. As wars, economic downturns, and political upheavals have challenged this nation's commitment to its ideals, these issues have come to the forefront again and again. Each time, they have been put under the lens of contemporary fears and needs. Each time, they have evoked different responses.

Free speech, immigration, and nation-building have all been reinterpreted during the past century under a variety of conditions, for a variety of reasons. In many instances, the results have demonstrated the best facets of the American experiment. In others, they have revealed an unappealing, even tragic, side. These resource books detail the ways that Americans have dealt with free speech, immigration, and nation-building over the course of recent history, for better and for worse. They present pivotal "Defining Moments" that illustrate both the brightest periods in our history and its darkest episodes.

At their center, these resource books are devoted to providing each student with the raw materials to evaluate each issue on his or her own. In each resource book, the student will find a wide array of primary materials: laws, poems, quotations, cartoons, speeches, editorials, and images. To help students interpret these historical documents and give them a solid grounding in the topic, secondary essays, glossaries, and background material are provided as well. This material, too, has been drawn from a great variety of sources: experts in diverse fields including education, political science, history, and literature.

Together, these primary and secondary sources form the building blocks for sets of classroom activities. These activities are designed to encourage students to analyze primary documents and to use their conclusions to evaluate the ways that free speech, immigration, and nation-building have been handled throughout past centuries. Students are asked to debate, to role play, and to write creatively about the historical materials. At the conclusion of the activity, the students are asked to judge the actions of the parties involved and to unravel the complexities within each issue.

Opening each resource book, you will find a series of essays designed to introduce students to each topic. The first essay is a broad issue overview. The second essay is more specific and chronological. Next, the resource books present two "Defining Moments" — landmark historical events that illustrate the nature of debate on each topic. Each Defining Moment section begins with detailed background information. Then you will find the classroom activities, with instructions and a list of materials needed to complete them. These materials, primary sources and reference pieces, follow each classroom activity section. The activities are broken down into parts, each one designed to challenge the students' assumptions and lead them to different conclusions. The last portion of the activity asks the students to assess both the Defining Moment and the issue at large.

In partnering to compile the *Triumph & Tragedy* series of resource books, ABC-CLIO and National History Day, Inc. continue their commitment to challenging students with historical material that both celebrates and complicates our concept of the national heritage. By combining quality research with active learning, we hope to bring the excitement of lively history and participatory civics to your classroom.

BECKY SNYDER
President, Schools Publisher
ABC-CLIO

CATHY GORN
Executive Director
National History Day

Preface

For young adults, it is simply not enough to read texts about vital issues at the heart of American citizenship. Like the generations before them, our students are going to grapple with these topics in their lifetimes. They need to prepare by turning a critical eye upon the histories of free speech, immigration, and nation-building. Their understanding of the past will help them to make sense of the present and to make informed decisions in the future. Teaching students to examine these issues as related to the theme of *Triumph & Tragedy* will provide a framework with which to push past the antiquated view of history as mere facts and dates and drill down into historical content to develop perspective and understanding.

Students sometimes learn history fast and without meaning. The discipline is vast, and the current educational climate emphasizes coverage of content over depth. Class design is often determined by time periods and approached chronologically. But without a guiding framework, students are abandoned to isolated pieces of historical information. A theme redefines how history is learned. Instead of concentrating on the whole century or a broad topic, students are invited to stop and analyze a smaller event, a part of the story, and place it in the context of the whole. Teaching with a theme ensures that students are not overwhelmed with the sheer vastness of the field but are invited to look deeply into a manageable portion of it instead.

Triumph & Tragedy provides students with a lens to read history, an organizational structure that helps them to place information in the correct context, and finally, gives them the ability to see connections over time. We invite your students to extend their study of free speech, immigration, and nation-building by engaging in active research and presentation.

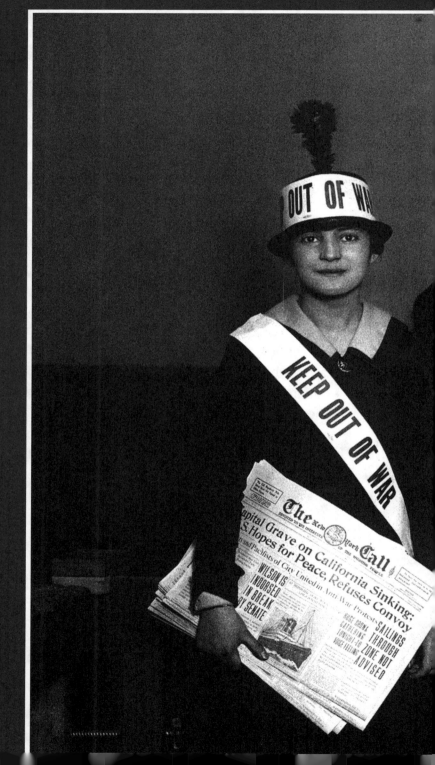

Well Chosen Words, Well Chosen Circumstances

Introduction

Bettmann/Corbis

Time & Life Pictures/
Getty Images

Civil Rights and the First Amendment

Author

DR. CHARLES MULLIN
UNIVERSITY OF
CALIFORNIA
SANTA BARBARA

When the Constitution of the United States was submitted to Congress for ratification in 1787, some states were hesitant to approve this philosophical blueprint without an explicit guarantee of certain rights. Having only recently severed their bond with what they saw as a tyrannical centralized authority, the fledgling states were reluctant to allow the federal government to exercise too much power over the citizens of the new United States. In response to these fears, a series of amendments was written: a Bill of Rights. It spelled out, more specifically than the Constitution itself, a number of rights possessed by citizens that the federal government could not abridge. Originally, the states proposed twelve amendments to the Constitution for inclusion in this Bill of Rights. But by 1791, the number was reduced to ten, and these amendments were ratified by the required number of states.

The First Amendment to the Constitution reads as follows:

Congress shall make no law respecting an establishment of religion, or prohibiting the free exercise thereof; or abridging the freedom of speech, or of the press; or the right of the people peaceably to assemble, and to petition the Government for a redress of grievances.

Despite its apparently unambiguous language, the precise meaning of the First Amendment has been the subject of philosophical debate and judicial interpretation for more than two centuries. With regard to freedom of speech, some scholars and jurists take an "absolutist" view of the First Amendment. They assert that "no law" means "no law," and so any government restriction of individual expression is unconstitutional by definition. However, most analysts acknowledge that there may be times when, in the interest of national security or public safety, some government regulation of individual expression may be warranted. Under these circumstances, the limitation of free speech is deemed constitutional.

By reviewing key free speech issues and the court cases they have generated over the last century, we can examine the ways in which legislators, scholars, and the legal community have sought to balance the protection of individual expression with social and governmental interests.

Sedition

Governments will always face a certain degree of criticism. They must be willing and able to absorb some amount of anti-government rhetoric. However, during wartime and other moments of national stress, the voices of dissent may become louder and more forceful. As a result, the government may grow increasingly willing to restrict speech that it feels might threaten national security or other legitimate government interests. In the 20th century, several events brought these forces into play, such as the socialist opposition to World War I, the perceived threat of communism in the 1950s, and the tumultuous political climate of the 1960s. At each step, the Supreme Court has sought to determine at what point anti-government expression may be lawfully constrained.[1]

Central to this discussion has been the formulation of the "clear and present danger" test. This allows the government to restrict speech that threatens to trigger serious harm to the nation that the government has a right to prevent. Over the years, the Court's concept of this test has become far more tolerant and protective of anti-government rhetoric than was initially the case. Today, speech is punishable only if it directly incites immediate lawless action (as opposed to advocacy of illegal action at some distant time). Furthermore, it must be deemed likely to produce such action.

Assaultive Speech
Fighting Words and Hate Speech

The government has a right—indeed, an obligation—to prevent breaches of the peace such as fights or riots. Since some forms of speech, like epithets and insults, may well provoke violence, governments have sometimes sought to criminalize expression of this type. The Supreme Court has had to delicately craft an interpretation of the First Amendment in this area that balances the government's interest in preserving public order with the individual's right to self-expression.

In a 1942 case,[2] the Supreme Court developed a "fighting words" doctrine. It has been sharpened a number of times since its inception, and now narrowly permits the government to punish speech delivered in a face-to-face confrontation if it is likely to create an immediate breach of the peace.

Interestingly, the "fighting words" doctrine has been frequently misapplied over the years in unsuccessful attempts to criminalize all manner of potentially offensive speech. Everything from hate speech to flag desecration has been wrongly described as "fighting words" by those who seek to regulate these forms of communication.

Hate speech (that is, language that abuses or insults a particular race, religion, gender, sexual-orientation, etc.) is deemed offensive by many and believed to contribute little of value to the intellectual marketplace. Nevertheless, speech does not lose protection merely because it is unpopular.[3] Hate speech typically involves categories of speech (for example, political, social, religious, or philosophical) that the First Amendment was designed to protect. In any case, hate speech rarely involves the "face-to-face" confrontational context demanded by the "fighting words" doctrine.

Along these lines, it is also worth noting that "speech codes," such as those at some college campuses that punish students for engaging in disfavored speech, are presumptively unconstitutional. Such codes restrict social discourse to ideas that meet with government approval. This restriction is deemed particularly egregious in college settings, traditionally regarded as arenas for the robust exchange of ideas.

Moralistic Regulation
Obscenity and Indecency

"Obscenity," because it has been characterized as contributing nothing of value to public discussion, has never been afforded First Amendment protection. So the question brought before the Court over the last century has been: *What is the appropriate definition of obscenity?*, rather than: *Under what conditions may this form of expression be regulated?*

As late as the 1930s, the definition of obscenity in America was so broad that James Joyce's literary masterpiece *Ulysses* was declared obscene because of some suggestive passages (a finding that was later overturned by a District Court judge[4]). Obscenity cases started reaching the Supreme Court in the 1950s. By the early 1970s,[5] the Court had formulated a definition of obscenity that more narrowly targeted the kind of sexually explicit content often labeled "obscene." The Court improved on previous definitions by declaring that something could only be deemed obscene if a jury, considering the entirety of the work—not just selected portions—found that the material in question exceeded relevant contemporary community standards of objectionable and that it lacked any serious literary, artistic, political, or scientific value. This approach empowered communities to develop and maintain their own local standards of decency rather than having those standards dictated by national preferences or even by the cultural norms of other communities.

"Indecency" is not the same thing as obscenity. Depending how the term is used, it might refer to municipal codes regulating adult businesses and nude dancing. But more commonly, "indecency" refers to the kind of "racy" expression associated with broadcasting personalities like Howard Stern.[6] To be found legally indecent, the expression in question must be broadcast between 6 AM and 10 PM, and must describe in "patently offensive" terms sexual or excretory activities or organs. Importantly, and for reasons that are too complicated to describe here, this law only applies to "over-the-air" broadcasting. This means that content that only reaches audiences via satellites or cables is free from such constraint. Unlike obscenity cases, which involve judgments rendered by juries, indecency complaints are handled by the Federal Communication Commission (FCC).

Conclusion

The three general areas just outlined—sedition, assaultive speech, and moralistic regulation—cover only a portion of the First Amendment landscape, but they allow us to extract some general interpretive philosophies:

Firstly, scholars and jurists place a high value on the concept of the intellectual marketplace. Rather than driving potentially offensive or harmful speech out of circulation through censorship, free speech advocates favor the inclusion of as many voices as possible, trusting the audience to distill wisdom from the ensuing competing ideas.

Secondly, speech regulations are permissible under certain narrowly defined circumstances (sometimes called "time, place, and manner" restrictions), but they may not be based on whether or not the government approves of the content. This "content neutrality" principle not only prohibits the government from censoring expression because it disagrees with the message, but it also prevents the government from forcing individuals to express views the government wants to promote.

Thirdly, for a speech restriction to be upheld, the government must provide convincing evidence that the speech in question, if unrestrained, will lead to some sort of injury that the government is legitimately empowered to prevent. This is a very difficult issue (what, for instance, are the harms associated with indecent speech or obscenity?). The potential harms the government seeks to prevent must be balanced against the certain harm done to the spirit of free speech with each regulatory action.

Sources

1. Landmark sedition cases from the World War I era include *Schenck v. United States* (1919); *Abrams v. United States* (1919); *Gitlow v. New York* (1925); and *Whitney v. California* (1927). Two important sedition cases from the 1950s are *Dennis v. United States* (1951) and *Yates v. United States* (1957). The most recent important landmark case in the area of sedition is *Brandenburg v. Ohio* (1969).

2. *Chaplinsky v. New Hampshire* (1942).

3. An illuminating case in this area is *R.A.V. v. St. Paul* (1992).

4. *United States v. One Book Called "Ulysses"* (1933) [State District Court of New York].

5. Three important cases in this area are *Roth v. United States* (1957); *Book Named "John Cleland's Memoirs of a Woman of Pleasure" v. Attorney General of Massachusetts* (1966); and *Miller v. California* (1973).

6. Important indecency-related cases include *FCC v. Pacifica Foundation* (1978), and *Action for Children's Television v. FCC* (1995) [DC Circuit Court].

Language and
the Law

Throughout History

1791–1917
Free Speech Ignored

Author

DR. CHARLES MULLIN
UNIVERSITY OF CALIFORNIA SANTA BARBARA

The primary function of a doctrine of free speech is to promote democracy by protecting criticism of the government. It is thus somewhat surprising that, for more than a century following its ratification, the First Amendment offered little impediment to governmental constraints on seditious speech.

A political cartoon from 1864 entitled "The Grave of the Union" shows President Abraham Lincoln and his cabinet "burying" civil rights "killed" during the Civil War. These included free speech and freedom of the press.

Corbis

For example, in 1798, President John Adams and his allies in Congress enacted the Alien and Sedition Acts. The Acts were designed to stifle criticism of Adams. The Alien Act made it easier to deport foreigners living in the United States, many of whom openly supported Adams' opponent, Thomas Jefferson. The Sedition Act punished "false, scandalous and malicious writing" against the government. While nobody would defend false information as a welcome contribution to the political process, scholars and jurists alike have generally agreed that if the press becomes skittish and timid under the threat of punishment, it cannot competently and enthusiastically fulfill its "watchdog" function with respect to governmental behavior.

John Adams, second president of the United States. Adams and his allies passed the Alien and Sedition Acts in 1798. These were the first laws abridging free speech enacted in the nation's history.

Library of Congress

Freedom of expression did not fare any better during the antebellum and Civil War eras of the mid-1800s. Some state governments passed legislation designed to punish the expression of abolitionist arguments. During the war, both the Union and Confederacy actively persecuted critics of their respective governments and war efforts.

1917–1950s
Free Speech Defined

The modern era of First Amendment jurisprudence regarding sedition really began around the time of World War I. During this period the Supreme Court considered a number of cases (such as *Schenck v. United States*, 1919; *Abrams v. United States,* 1919; *Gitlow v. New York,* 1925; and *Whitney v. California,* 1927) that involved either a violation of the Espionage Act of 1917 and Sedition Act of 1918 or that involved socialist calls for class revolution. In all these cases, the Supreme Court asked the same question: *At what point does seditious speech become sufficiently threatening to legitimate governmental interests that it may be punished without offending the First Amendment?*

During this period, Justices Oliver Wendell Holmes and Louis Brandeis argued that political dissent enhanced the intellectual marketplace. It should only be abridged if the speech in question posed a "clear and present danger" that the government is required to address. The inevitable question then became: *How serious, likely, and imminent must a specified threat be before one can declare that the "clear and present danger" test has been met?*

Louis Brandeis became famous for his dissenting opinions in support of liberal causes while an associate justice of the U.S. Supreme Court.

Library of Congress

As a practical matter, the Supreme Court ended up resolving sedition cases of this period by essentially employing what is called the "bad tendency" test. It permits restriction of speech that the government regards as having a *tendency* to lead to illegal activity. Since the "bad tendency" test offers far less protection for dissent than does the "clear and present danger" test, the major sedition convictions in this era were upheld by the Supreme Court.

The Supreme Court revisited this territory in the 1950s in cases involving communists. Lower courts convicted them of violating the 1940 Smith Act, which punished speech that advocated the "necessity, desirability, or propriety" of overthrowing the U.S. government by force.

In *Dennis v. United States,* the Court upheld an American Communist Party member's conviction under the Smith Act, noting that the expression in question represented *advocacy* of forceful overthrow rather than merely a *discussion* of the issue. The Court also felt that the "clear and present danger" test did not require the government to wait until the very last moment before the commission of an illegal act before it acted to deter it. By the end of the 1950s, however, the Court adopted a more protective attitude toward dissent by declaring in a 1957 case *(Yates v. United States)* that speech only posed a "clear and present danger" if it advocated *direct illegal action,* rather than merely advocating an *abstract doctrine.*

Bettman/Corbis

Six members of the American Communist Party indicted for sedition under the Smith Act, July 21, 1948. Third from the left is the party's general secretary, Eugene Dennis. The case was appealed, but the Supreme Court upheld his conviction under the "clear and present danger" test.

1960s–Present
Free Speech Explored

The Supreme Court's increasing tolerance for seditious speech reached its peak with the 1969 case *Brandenburg v. Ohio*, which involved the conviction of a Ku Klux Klan member whose vague threats during a rally violated an Ohio state law prohibiting advocacy of "unlawful methods of . . . accomplishing industrial or political reform." In overturning the conviction and invalidating the state law, the Court formulated an "incitement standard" whereby seditious speech could only be punished if it is "directed to inciting or producing imminent lawless action *and is likely to incite or produce such actions*" (emphasis added). The incitement standard protects even threatening speech if it seems that the speaker is "blowing off steam," rather than directly encouraging unlawful action.

Ku Klux Klan burning a cross in Swainsboro, Georgia. The Supreme Court ruled in Brandenburg v. Ohio *(1969) that even offensive speech was protected by the First Amendment, provided that speech was not a prompt to immediate lawless action. This case overturned the standards imposed by* Schenck v. United States *(1919).*

In the fifty years between *Schenck* and *Brandenburg,* the Supreme Court's interpretation of the First Amendment broadened to the point where it is hard to imagine any conviction for seditious speech being upheld today. Many of the principles developed in sedition case rulings during these years have been applied to other forms of political dissent, such as flag desecration. The American flag is a venerated symbol of our country and critics have found that destroying the flag sends a powerful emotional message. Many state legislatures have passed laws over the years designed to criminalize flag desecration. In the 1989 case of *Texas v. Johnson*, the Supreme Court considered the constitutionality of one such statute. Gregory Lee Johnson, a member of the Revolutionary Communist Youth Brigade, burned a flag as part

1960s–Present
Free Speech Explored, cont.

of a demonstration against the policies of the Reagan administration in 1984. Concerns raised by this case highlight some of the remaining unanswered questions regarding free speech:

Because flag burning typically takes place in near-riot conditions in which passions run high, could Texas' law be deemed constitutional as a reasonable way to prevent a breach of the peace?

Because Johnson had other legal ways to express himself and insert his ideas into the intellectual marketplace (such as by carrying a sign, or by giving a speech), might this law be acceptable because Johnson is only prevented from using one particular communicative method?

The stated purpose of the Texas law was to preserve the flag's symbolic value, but does preventing flag burning accomplish this goal? Might a better way to promote respect for the flag be to embrace the freedoms it represents that make it a symbol worthy of respect?

A majority of the Supreme Court in this case agreed that the First Amendment guaranteed Johnson's right to express dissent by burning the flag. But the questions raised by the decision will no doubt return in future free speech cases.

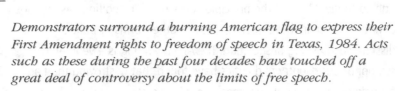

Demonstrators surround a burning American flag to express their First Amendment rights to freedom of speech in Texas, 1984. Acts such as these during the past four decades have touched off a great deal of controversy about the limits of free speech.

Time & Life Pictures/Getty Images

Sources

Abrams v. United States, 250 US 616 (1919).

Action for Children's Television v. FCC, 59 F3d 1249 (DC Cir 1995).

Brandenburg v. Ohio, 395 US 444 (1969).

Chaplinsky v. New Hampshire, 315 US 568 (1942).

Dennis v. United States, 341 US 494 (1951).

FCC v. Pacifica Foundation, 438 US 726 (1978).

Gitlow v. New York, 268 US 652 (1925).

Book Named "John Cleland's Memoirs of a Woman of Pleasure" v. Attorney General of Massachusetts, 383 US 413 (1966).

Miller v. California, 413 US 15 (1973).

R.A.V. v. St. Paul, 505 US 377 (1992).

Roth v. United States, 354 US 476 (1957).

Schenck v. United States, 249 US 47 (1919).

Texas v. Johnson, 491 US 397 (1989).

United States v. One Book Called "Ulysses," 5 F Supp 182 (SDNY 1933).

Whitney v. California, 274 US 357 (1927).

Yates v. United States, 354 US 298 (1957).

Words, War, and the Workplace

Defining Moment

Words, War, and the Workplace

Schenck v. United States was a landmark case in the history of free speech legislation in this country. It has influenced thinking on the subject for the last century and will no doubt continue to do so. To understand the case, it is necessary to understand the world that produced it. The tone of the times played a significant role in the way it unfolded. America's industrial development is at the heart of the issue. In the early 20th century, the workers who made the nation's growth possible often did not receive adequate pay for their work. Labor unions, designed to help workers to negotiate better conditions, were growing in number, size, and power. Lawmakers were deciding how companies and unions should interact, passing laws to regulate their conduct. Still, there were a number of ugly clashes between employers and employees during the generations preceding World War I. Such violence was very unnerving for America, a nation that prided itself on providing equal opportunity for all.

THIS MUST NOT BE!

Library of Congress

Political cartoon of man (Congress) driving woman (Liberty) down steps of U.S. Capitol with whip labeled "Espionage Bill." In 1917, Congress passed the Espionage Act in an effort to protect the nation from domestic treachery while it prepared to join World War I in Europe. In its original draft, the bill outlawed even criticism of the government.

The political philosophy of socialism grew out of the plight of industrial workers and became intertwined with workers' movements. It originated in Europe and quickly spread to the United States. Socialist labor leaders like American Eugene v. Debs wanted to improve the lot of the workingman by redistributing wealth and power. Some were even more radical; speaker Emma Goldman preached the violent overthrow of national governments, which she saw as the props of economic and social corruption. This was not just talk since actual violence arose from these ideas. A political radical named Leon Czolgosz assassinated President William McKinley in 1901. In short, the socialists seemed about to throw the United States into chaos during the first decades of the 20th century.

Socialist labor leader Eugene Debs delivers an anti-war speech —
June 16, 1918 in Canton, Ohio. For making this speech, Debs was
prosecuted under the Sedition Act of 1918 and sentenced to ten
years in prison.

When World War I began in Europe, most socialists loudly protested the war in general and American participation in particular. America was unsettled on the issue of war even without socialist agitation. The nation was divided between the desire to remain isolated from European events and the desire to assert her might and to protect her interests by intervening. Somewhat reluctantly, the United States had begun to prepare troops for overseas fighting by early 1917. But the question of going to war remained fraught with political tension. To the government and citizens alike, it seemed that the Socialists were attempting to sink the controversial war effort while calling for the destruction of American society. The nation felt that it was heading for disaster: weakened by enemies at home as it attempted to face enemies abroad.

Fear, perhaps even a touch of paranoia, prompted Congress to pass the Espionage Act of 1917 and the Sedition Act of 1918. The Acts criminalized anti-government words and deeds, particularly in wartime. Precisely at this moment, an American socialist, Charles Schenck, sent 15,000 anti-war pamphlets through the mail to potential draftees. Schenck urged the men to refuse to fight just as the United States was preparing to send troops overseas. Although the pamphlet did not advocate violence, the Espionage and Sedition Acts had outlawed actions that aided the enemies of the United States. A peaceful call to draft-dodge fell under this heading. For interfering with military recruitment, Schenck was charged with sedition under the Espionage Act. The

Words, War, and the Workplace cont.

Supreme Court became involved because Schenck's arrest pitted an individual's right to speak freely against the nation's right to look after its own interests. Free speech was very much at issue.

New York Times *account of Supreme Court ruling in* Schenck v. United States *in 1919.*

The unanimous U.S. Supreme Court decision in *Schenck v. United States* (1919) was written by Justice Oliver Wendell Holmes. He upheld Schenck's conviction and the constitutionality of the Espionage Act. Although he noted that Schenck's actions would have been protected in ordinary times and places, he said that they were not protected in this case because this time and place were extraordinary: the nation was going off to war and dangerous ideas were threatening the country's very existence. Holmes wrote, "When a nation is at war many things that might be said in time of peace are such a hindrance to its effort that their utterance will not be endured so long as men fight and that no court could regard them as protected by any constitutional right." To support his point, Holmes made a famous analogy, saying that a person did not have the right to shout fire falsely in a crowded theater. What he meant was that words needed to be judged within their context. A person could shout "fire!" in an empty room and cause no harm to anyone. A person yelling it in a crowd, causing a fatal stampede, made for another case altogether. Holmes said that Congress had the right to legislate against words or actions that posed "a clear and present danger" to the nation's existence.

Oliver Wendell Holmes and the Supreme Court set a precedent with the *Schenck* decision that would influence rulings in free speech cases for decades to come. The "clear and present danger" test was revived a few years later in the case of *Gitlow v. New York* (1925). In this case, a political radical named Benjamin Gitlow published a pamphlet called "The Left Wing Manifesto" that called for the overthrow of the U.S. government. In this case, the Court expanded its position on free speech when Justice Edward Sanford devised the "dangerous" or "bad tendency" test and applied it to the case instead. With this test, Sanford acknowledged that freedom of speech and the press were protected, *except* when they expressly advocated the overthrow of the government. With the *Gitlow* decision, it became clear that the U.S. Supreme Court was thinking seriously about the definition of free speech in America and considering how to best protect both it and the material interest. However, "clear and present danger" remained the standard against which free speech cases would be measured for the next few decades. That is, until another war — Vietnam — brought these issues before the Court again and a new era in free speech legislation began.

Words, War, and the Workplace

Lesson Overview

This lesson will take place in two stages. In Part I, the teacher will lead the students in a group discussion about the meaning of the First Amendment and the Espionage Act of 1917. The teacher will pose questions to the class about what behaviors might be deemed "seditious" in this time period and what behaviors might be acceptable.

In Part II, the students will enact a mock trial with Schenck as the defendant.

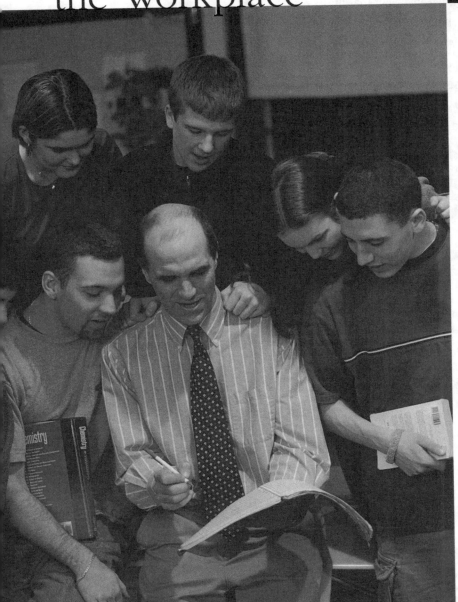

Authors

CHRIS MULLIN
SANTA YNEZ VALLEY
UNION HIGH SCHOOL

BRETT PIERSMA
SANTA YNEZ VALLEY
UNION HIGH SCHOOL

Lesson Plan Part I
Class Discussion

In the first portion of this activity, the teacher should provide the students with the handout of the First Amendment to the Constitution (this document can also be projected as a slide or written out on the board). The teacher should begin by reminding the students that the First Amendment is a part of the U.S. Constitution and was added in 1791, more than 120 years before World War I.

Now the teacher should ask a student to volunteer to read the amendment out loud for the class. Once the student has finished reading, the teacher should go through the document slowly and see if there are any protections that the students do not necessarily understand. Examples might included assembly, worship, and so forth. The teacher should then focus the discussion specifically on the freedom of speech (last two questions). Guide questions might include the following:

- What specific actions does this amendment protect?
- What is the government prohibited from doing?
- Does it surprise you to see any of these protections included in the 1790s?
- Do you think our citizens enjoy these rights today?
- Is the government ever criticized for violating these rights?
- Do you have absolute freedom of speech? At school? In public?
- What limits do you think you have on your freedom of speech?

Once the teacher has completed the discussion on the right to free speech, he or she should pass out the excerpt from the Espionage Act of 1917 and ask a student to read it out loud. Once the student is done, the teacher should direct the discussion to how war affects citizens' freedom of expression and the government's possible justifications for abridging those rights. Possible questions include the following:

- What kind of free speech activity do you think this federal law prohibits?
- What do you think sedition means?
- Why do you think this law was passed?
- Does this law violate the First Amendment? Why? Why not?

Now that the students have completed a discussion of both the First Amendment and the Espionage Act, it is time to begin the trial.

Activity
LESSON PLAN PART I

For this portion of the activity, students will need copies of:

PRIMARY SOURCES
- Excerpt from the First Amendment to the Constitution, p. 31
- Excerpt from the Espionage Act of 1917, p. 32

Lesson Plan Part II
The Trial

The teacher should begin the trial by giving a brief historical description of the circumstances surrounding the case. Charles Schenck was a man who, during wartime, was arrested for distributing pamphlets encouraging men to resist the draft. He was arrested and prosecuted for sedition under the Espionage Act of 1917. The teacher should distribute copies of Schenck's anti-war pamphlet for students to read.

The teacher now divides the class into eight teams of three. Four of these teams will attempt to prove Schenck guilty of violating the Espionage Act. The remaining four teams will attempt to prove that his actions were within the law and protected by the First Amendment. The remaining students in the class will play the role of a jury, ultimately ruling innocent or guilty based on the arguments and facts presented.

Once the teams of three have been created, hand out Roles Sheets and Fact Pattern Sheets. Students in each team must select a role (Scholar, Writer, or Presenter). The Scholar is responsible for analyzing the documents and formulating arguments for the presentation. The Writer is responsible for writing the 200-word formal presentation based on the Scholar's input. The Presenter is responsible for reading the argument in front of the class in a commanding and compelling manner. The Fact Pattern Sheets contain instructions on how to formulate arguments and questions to think about.

The remaining students are given the Jury Instructions sheet. As a group, they must create a rubric for judging the presentations and facts given.

Allow students thirty minutes to prepare.

Once they are ready, the Presenters from the Prosecution groups give their speeches one by one. Then, the Presenters from the Defense groups give their speeches one by one. Meanwhile, the Jury takes notes and grades each speech based on the rubric the Jury developed.

Activity
LESSON PLAN PART II

For this portion of the activity, students will need copies of:

ACTIVITY SHEETS
- Activity Sheet 1, p. 26 (24 copies)
- Activity Sheet 2, p. 27 (12 copies)
- Activity Sheet 3, p. 28 (12 copies)
- Activity Sheet 4, p. 29 (12 copies)

PRIMARY SOURCES
- Excerpt from the First Amendment to the Constitution, p. 31
- Excerpt from the Espionage Act of 1917, p. 32
- Excerpt from Supreme Court ruling by Oliver Wendell Holmes, p. 33
- Pamphlet distributed by Schenck, pp. 34–35
- Photo 1, p. 36
- Photo 2, p. 37

Once all speeches have been given, the Jury deliberates in private (with the teacher as Judge) and tallies their scores. Then, the announcement is made as to guilt or innocence.

Next, the students are given Oliver Wendell Holmes' "clear and present danger" ruling. The teacher instructs one student to read it aloud to the class while the others follow along. The teacher then holds a discussion covering the implications of this ruling (as creating the "clear and present danger" test for future restrictions on speech). Possible questions include the following:

- What actions might constitute a "clear and present danger" to the government?
- Can you think of examples in the news of people engaging in such actions?
- Do you think that the government should have more power to abridge speech during war?

Finally, students are given copies of the two photographs, Photo 1 and Photo 2. Based upon their study of the other materials and their discussions, they should evaluate what they see. Some possible questions might include:

- Are these people committing sedition?
- Is a mass activity more influential than that of individuals?
- If you were a government official, how would you respond to both of these situations?

Activity Sheet 1
Roles Sheets

SCHOLAR

As the scholar of the group, your job is to work with your team to find quotes and determine arguments for your speech. You must make sure your group goes through the entire document systematically and formulates logical positions on the issues.

WRITER

You are responsible for using the Scholar's and Presenter's ideas to write the speech. You must make sure that your sentences flow logically and are worded effectively so that your Presenter will be effective. Also, write neatly so that the Presenter can read it.

PRESENTER

You will present the speech your team has written to the Jury and to the rest of the class. You must help formulate the speech and make sure you can read the writing and understand the arguments you will make. Try to memorize a significant portion of your speech so that you will not be reading directly from the page.

Activity Sheet 2
Fact Pattern for Prosecution

INSTRUCTIONS

As a team, you are going to develop a case for convicting Schenck. He is on trial for violation of the Espionage Act of 1917. You will develop and write a 200-word argument that your Presenter will read to the Jury. As you prepare this speech, select at least two main ideas that you will emphasize and repeat throughout the speech. Consider these issues as you plan your prosecution:

• Does the First Amendment protect all forms of free speech in any circumstances?

• Are there any types of expression that should be illegal? Why? Why not?

• Is there clear evidence that Schenck has violated the Espionage Act of 1917?

• What does Schenck's pamphlet specifically say that is in direct violation of the Espionage Act?

Find quotes from each document to prove your case. Be aware also that your opponents will probably try to say that the First Amendment overrules the provisions of the Espionage Act because it is part of the U.S. Constitution. How will you address that issue?

Activity Sheet 3
Fact Pattern for Defense

INSTRUCTIONS

As a team, you are going to develop a defense for Charles Schenck. He is on trial for violation of the Espionage Act of 1917. You will develop and write a 200-word argument that your Presenter will read to the Jury. As you prepare this speech, select at least two main ideas that you will emphasize and repeat throughout the speech. Consider these issues as you plan your defense:

- Why does the Constitution protect free expression of ideas?
- Is the Espionage Act a violation of the First Amendment?
- Which takes precedence, the First Amendment or the Espionage Act?
- What does Schenck's pamphlet specifically say that is in direct violation of the Espionage Act? Is there clear evidence?

Find quotes from each document to prove your case. Be aware also that your opponents will probably try to say that the Espionage Act is vital to protect the United States and that it does not violate the Constitution. How will you address that issue?

Activity Sheet 4
Jury Instructions

While the small groups are working on their speeches, you are going to develop a grading scale that you will use to evaluate the arguments of your fellow students. Make a list of five descriptions (Grade 1 for the weakest argument and Grade 5 for the strongest argument) and use them to judge the statements you are about to hear. For example you might write:

Grade 1: It is not made clear why the team feels Schenck is guilty. There are no quotations from either the Espionage Act or from Schenck's pamphlet itself. They do not base their argument on the letter of the law.

Grade 2

_____

_____

_____

Grade 3

_____

_____

_____

Grade 4

_____

_____

_____

Grade 5

_____

_____

_____

As each small group comes up to present, each Juror should judge the arguments independently and use his or her template to compare notes. Once they have all shared their opinions on the various arguments, they will reach a decision in the case, declaring Schenck guilty or innocent.

Primary Sources

Words, War, and the Workplace

Excerpt
from the First Amendment to the Constitution

Congress shall make no law respecting an establishment of religion, or
prohibiting the free exercise thereof; or abridging the freedom of
speech, or of the press; or the right of the people peaceably to
assemble, and to petition the Government for a redress of grievances.

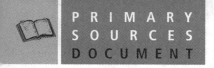

Excerpt
from the Espionage Act of 1917

SECTION 3

Whoever, when the United States is at war, shall willfully make or convey false reports or false statements with intent to interfere with the operation or success of the military or naval forces of the United States or to promote the success of its enemies and whoever when the United States is at war, shall willfully cause or attempt to cause insubordination, disloyalty, mutiny, refusal of duty, in the military or naval forces of the United States, or shall willfully obstruct the recruiting or enlistment service of the United States, to the injury of the service or of the United States, shall be punished by a fine of not more than $10,000 or imprisonment for not more than twenty years, or both.

SECTION 4

If two or more persons conspire to violate the provisions of section two or three of this title, and one or more of such persons does any act to effect the object of the conspiracy, each of the parties to such conspiracy shall be punished as in said sections provided in the case of the doing of the act the accomplishment of which is the object of such conspiracy. Except as above provided conspiracies to commit offenses under this title shall be punished as provided by section thirty-seven of the Act to codify, revise, and amend the penal laws of the United States approved March fourth, nineteen hundred and nine.

Excerpt
from Supreme Court Ruling
by Oliver Wendell Holmes

We admit that in many places and in ordinary times the defendants in saying all that was said in the circular would have been within their constitutional rights. But the character of every act depends upon the circumstances in which it is done. The most stringent protection of free speech would not protect a man in falsely shouting fire in a theatre and causing a panic. It does not even protect a man from an injunction against uttering words that may have all the effect of force. The question in every case is whether the words used are used in such circumstances and are of such a nature as to create a clear and present danger that they will bring about the substantive evils that Congress has a right to prevent. It is a question of proximity and degree. When a nation is at war many things that might be said in time of peace are such a hindrance to its effort that their utterance will not be endured so long as men fight and that no Court could regard them as protected by any constitutional right.

Pamphlet
Distributed by Schenck

Example of two-sided pamphlet sent by socialist Charles Schenck to 15,000 potential draftees in an effort to halt World War I recruitment. Schenck was prosecuted under the Espionage Act of 1917. His conviction was upheld in *Schenck v. United States* (1919), the first landmark free speech case in American history.

ASSERT YOUR RIGHTS!

Article 6, Section 2, of the Constitution of the United States says: "This Constitution shall be the *supreme law of the Land.*"

Article 1 (Amendment) says: "Congress shall make no law respecting an establishment of religion, or *prohibiting the free exercise thereof.*"

Article 9 (Amendment) says: "The enumeration in the Constitution of certain rights, shall not be construed to deny or disparge others retained by the people."

The Socialist Party says that any individual or officers of the law entrusted with the administration of conscription regulations, violate the provisions of the United States Constitution, the Supreme Law of the Land, when they refuse to recognize your right to assert your opposition to the draft.

If you are conscientiously opposed to war, if you believe in the commandment "thou shalt not kill," then that is your religion, and you shall not be prohibited from the free exercise thereof.

In exempting clergymen and members of the Society of Friends (popularly called Quakers) from active military service, the examination boards have discriminated against you.

If you do not assert and support your rights, you are helping to "deny or disparage rights" which it is the solemn duty of all citizens and residents of the United States to retain.

Here in this city of Philadelphia was signed the immortal Declaration of Independence. As a citizen of "the cradle of American Liberty" you are doubly charged with the duty of upholding the rights of the people.

Will you let cunning politicians and a mercenary capitalist press wrongly and untruthfully mould your thoughts? Do not forget your right to elect officials who are opposed to conscription.

In lending tacit or silent consent to the conscription law, in neglecting to assert your rights, you are (whether unknowingly or not) helping to condone and support a most infamous and insidious conspiracy to abridge and destroy the sacred and cherished rights of a free people. **You are a citizen, not a subject!** You delegate your power to the officers of the law to be used for your good and welfare, not against you.

They are your servants. Not your masters. Their wages come from the expenses of government which you pay. Will you allow them to unjustly rule you? The fathers who fought and bled to establish a free and independent nation here in America were so opposed to the militarism of the old world from which they had escaped; so keenly alive to the dangers and hardships they had undergone in fleeing from political, religious and military oppression, that they handed down to us "certain rights which must be retained by the people."

They held the spirit of militarism in such abhorrence and hate, they were so apprehensive of the formation of a military machine that would insidiously and secretly advocate the invasion of other lands, that they limited the power of Congress over the militia in providing only for the calling forth of "the militia to execute laws of the Union, suppress insurrections and repel invasions." (See general powers of Congress, Article 1, Section 8, Paragraph 15.)

No power was delegated to send our citizens away to foreign shores to shoot up the people of other lands, no matter what may be their internal or international disputes.

The people of this country did not vote in favor of war. At the last election they voted against war.

To draw this country into the horrors of the present war in Europe, to force the youth of our land into the shambles and bloody trenches of war-crazy nations, would be a crime the magnitude of which defies description. Words could not express the condemnation such cold-blooded ruthlessness deserves.

Will you stand idly by and see the Moloch of Militarism reach forth across the sea and fasten its tentacles upon this continent? Are you willing to submit to the degradation of having the Constitution of the United States treated as a "mere scrap of paper?"

Do you know that patriotism means a love for your country and not hate for others?

Will you be led astray by a propaganda of jingoism masquerading under the guise of patriotism?

No specious or plausible pleas about a "war for democracy" can becloud the issue. Democracy cannot be shot into a nation. It must come spontaneously and purely from within.

Democracy must come through liberal education. Upholders of military ideas are unfit teachers.

To advocate the persecution of other peoples through the prosecution of war is an insult to every good and wholesome American tradition.

"These are the times that try men's souls."

"Eternal vigilance is the price of liberty."

You are responsible. You must do your share to maintain, support and uphold the rights of the people of this country.

In this world crisis where do you stand? Are you with the forces of liberty and light or war and darkness?

(OVER)

LONG LIVE THE CONSTITUTION OF THE UNITED STATES

Wake Up, America!   Your Liberties Are in Danger!

The 13th Amendment, Section 1, of the Constitution of the United States says: "Neither slavery nor involuntary servitude, except as a punishment for crime whereof the party shall have been duly convicted, shall exist within the United States, or any place subject to their jurisdiction."

The Constitution of the United States is one of the greatest bulwarks of political liberty. It was born after a long, stubborn battle between king-rule and democracy. (We see little or no difference between arbitrary power under the name of a king and under a few misnamed "representatives.") In this battle the people of the United States established the principle that freedom of the individual and personal liberty are the most sacred things in life. Without them we become slaves.

For this principle the fathers fought and died. The establishment of this principle they sealed with their own blood. Do you want to see this principle abolished? Do you want to see despotism substituted in its stead? Shall we prove degenerate sons of illustrious sires?

The Thirteenth Amendment to the Constitution of the United States, quoted above, embodies this sacred idea. The Socialist Party says that this idea is violated by the Conscription Act. When you conscript a man and compel him to go abroad to fight against his will, you violate the most sacred right of personal liberty, and substitute for it what Daniel Webster called "despotism in its worst form."

A conscript is little better than a convict. He is deprived of his liberty and of his right to think and act as a free man. A conscripted citizen is forced to surrender his right as a citizen and become a subject. He is forced into involuntary servitude. He is deprived of the protection given him by the Constitution of the United States. He is deprived of all freedom of conscience in being forced to kill against his will.

Are you one who is opposed to war, and were you misled by the venal capitalist newspapers, or intimidated or deceived by gang politicians and registrars into believing that you would not be allowed to register your objection to conscription? Do you know that many citizens of Philadelphia insisted on their right to answer the famous question twelve, and went on record with their honest opinion of opposition to war, notwithstanding the deceitful efforts of our rulers and the newspaper press to prevent them from doing so? Shall it be said that the citizens of Philadelphia, the cradle of American liberty, are so lost to a sense of right and justice that they will let such monstrous wrongs against humanity go unchallenged?

In a democratic country each man must have the right to say whether he is willing to join the army. Only in countries where uncontrolled power rules can a despot force his subjects to fight. Such a man or men have no place in a democratic republic. This is tyrannical power in its worst form. It gives control over the life and death of the individual to a few men. There is no man good enough to be given such power.

Conscription laws belong to a bygone age. Even the people of Germany, long suffering under the yoke of militarism, are beginning to demand the abolition of conscription. Do you think it has a place in the United States? Do you want to see unlimited power handed over to Wall Street's chosen few in America? If you do not, join the Socialist Party in its campaign for the repeal of the Conscription Act. Write to your congressman and tell him you want the law repealed. Do not submit to intimidation. You have a right to demand the repeal of any law. Exercise your rights of free speech, peaceful assemblage and petitioning the government for a redress of grievances. Come to the headquarters of the Socialist Party, 1326 Arch street, and sign a petition to congress for the repeal of the Conscription Act. Help us wipe out this stain upon the Constitution!

Help us re-establish democracy in America.

Remember, "eternal vigilance is the price of liberty."

Down with autocracy!

Long live the Constitution of the United States! Long live the Republic!

Books on Socialism for Sale at

SOCIALIST PARTY BOOK STORE AND HEADQUARTERS

1326 ARCH ST. Phone, Filbert 3121

(OVER)

Photo 1
Anti-war Rally, World War I

Corbis

People gather in Union Square,
New York City, to protest the U.S.
involvement in World War I,
c. 1914. Anti-war sentiment was the
backdrop to legislation passed during
this period that abridged free speech.

Photo 2
American Isolationists or
Anti-War Protesters

Socialists Rose Cohn,

Dorothy Day, and

Charlotte Margolies

wear sashes stating

"Keep Out of War"

to protest U.S.

involvement

in World War I, c. 1917.

Bettmann/Corbis

Glossary Words, Ideas, or Movements
Words, War, and the Workplace

AUTOCRACY A community or country ruled by a single person or group with unlimited authority. An autocrat is one who exercises such power.

"BAD TENDENCY" TEST In addition to the "clear and present danger" test (meaning that Congress should restrict free speech only in cases where the speech constitutes a clear and present danger), courts often applied the "bad" or "dangerous tendency" test. This test, epitomized by the Supreme Court's decision in *Gitlow v. New York* (1925), allowed governmental suppression of speech thought to have a bad or dangerous tendency, like the overthrow of the government. Modern courts have interpreted the First Amendment in a way that provides greater leeway to speech that the government might fear.

CENSORSHIP IN THE EARLY 20TH CENTURY It was the development of alternative political ideologies and parties in the early 20th century that gave rise to the modern form of censorship, particularly the emergence of communism, socialism, and anarchism as mass movements throughout the world. The U.S. entry into World War I in 1917 ushered in a period of intense scrutiny of the flow of information in the press and public. Never before had the entire nation needed to mobilize for war. Accordingly, the federal government assumed a firm control over the economy and deemed any politically dissenting voice as a threat to national security. The passage of the Espionage Act of 1917 targeted political dissent in any form that "promote[d] the success of [our] enemies." Many people who advocated peace were sent to prison, some serving sentences of twenty years, because their pamphlets or articles might motivate soldiers to avoid war. Pacifists or anyone who questioned the government's wartime policies were widely viewed by the public with suspicion and were sometimes prosecuted for their views.

CIRCULAR In *Schenck v. United States*, Justice Oliver Wendell Holmes refers to Charles Schenck's pamphlet as a "circular." In the 19th century, "circular" became a common word to describe a notice or advertisement printed and copied to be distributed in large numbers. Today, we might describe Schenck's document as a pamphlet, flier, or poster.

CONSCRIPTION Compulsory service in the military; a draft.

CONTUMELY Insulting or degrading.

DESPOTISM Despotism is a name for an abusive government with absolute power, usually led by a single ruler called a despot.

ESPIONAGE The act of spying on one country for the good of another, often in time of war.

"ETERNAL VIGILANCE IS THE PRICE OF LIBERTY" Abolitionist Wendell Phillips spoke this phrase in a speech to the Massachusetts Anti-Slavery Society in January, 1852. Phillips is generally credited with the quote, but its root comes from a speech made by John Philpot Curran in Ireland in 1790, in which he said, "The condition upon which God hath given liberty to man is eternal vigilance." Nonetheless, it was Phillips' speech that resonated with anti-war demonstrators like Charles Schenck in the early 20th century. A brilliant orator, Phillips was famous as the "golden trumpet" of the abolitionist movement. He was also an early supporter of the labor movement, arguing that wage earners were as much the victims of corporate capital as slaves had been of slavery. "Eternal vigilance is the price of liberty—power is ever stealing from the many to the few," Phillips said to the crowd in 1852.

Glossary Words, Ideas, or Movements
Words, War, and the Workplace, cont.

"The manna of popular liberty must be gathered each day, or it is rotten. . . . The hand entrusted with power becomes, either from human depravity or *esprit du corps,* the necessary enemy of the people. Only by continual oversight can the democrat in office be prevented from hardening into a despot: only by unintermitted Agitation can a people be kept sufficiently awake to principle not to let liberty be smothered in material prosperity."

FREEDOM OF EXPRESSION Related to freedom of speech, freedom of expression is the right to express freely thoughts, ideas, or opinions.

HATE SPEECH Remarks can be specifically punished as hate speech when they arouse alarm or anger on the basis of race, color, creed, religion, or gender. Penalties for hate speech can be enhanced when victims are especially targeted because of such criteria.

ISOLATIONISM A term that describes a foreign policy of limited involvement in the world outside the home state. It entails avoidance of political and military commitments and requires specific criteria for intervention.

JINGOISM An attitude of belligerent nationalism that often denigrates the peoples of other countries and leads to war. The term was probably coined when 19th-century British war hawks sang these lyrics: "We don't want to fight, but by Jingo if we do, we've got the ships, we've got the men, we've got the money, too." As a result, the term *jingo* or *jingoism* has come to mean a blustering, chauvinistic form of patriotism.

LABOR MOVEMENT IN THE EARLY 20TH CENTURY A labor movement is an organization of a mass of workers who wish to forward their interests. In the United States, the labor movement began in the mid-19th century as the Industrial Revolution produced a large working class.

The early 20th century saw momentous change for organized labor, particularly in the way that Americans viewed its role in society. Investigative journalists called "muckrakers" heightened public awareness of the abuses of big business and indirectly fostered support for workers' demands. Other reform-minded Americans focused their efforts on improving workplace conditions. Thousands of workers joined labor unions and participated in strikes and protests. In some of those protests, police or company-hired security forces turned violent, which prompted mass outpourings of public sympathy for the workers.

However, at the same time that labor was gaining legitimacy, some Americans were questioning the aims and goals of unions. Unions—with their demands for workers' rights, collective bargaining, and government regulation—challenged unrestrained capitalism. Many feared that unions marked a dangerous trend toward Socialism, Communism, and even Anarchism. And in fact, activists such as Eugene V. Debs and William Haywood did seek to radicalize the American labor movement.

Organized labor declined in influence during the prosperous 1920s. But when the Great Depression devastated the American economy in the 1930s, wage cuts, layoffs, and plant closures led to violent strikes nationwide.

Glossary Words, Ideas, or Movements
Words, War, and the Workplace, cont.

"LIMITED POWER OF CONGRESS OVER THE MILITIA" Refers to the Second Amendment. Rather than permitting the federal government to establish a professional military to use at will, the Amendment implies that the individual states may establish citizen militias for defensive purposes only. Therefore, the establishment of a national army and navy to fight overseas might be construed as a violation of the Constitution.

MILITARISM The view that military power and efficiency is the supreme ideal of the state.

MUTINY Resistance or revolt against authority; usually associated with military disobedience. A grave crime, mutiny occurs when two or more people defect to the enemy or refuse to obey orders.

SCURRILOUS Vulgar, coarse, or abusive language.

SEDITION The act of making statements or committing acts designed to advocate the overthrow of a government.

SOCIALISM A political and social system in which the government owns major industries and controls the production of goods and the means of distribution. The major aim of Socialism is the creation of a classless society.

SOCIALISM IN AMERICA IN THE EARLY 20TH CENTURY
The Socialist movement arose in Europe to address the widening gap between rich and poor as the West underwent rapid industrial expansion. The movement quickly spread to the United States. The years 1900–1919 were the heyday of American socialism, as the Socialist Party gained adherents and became a viable third party. From a few thousand scattered members in 1901, the party grew to 40,000 strong by 1908.

During World War I, European and American socialists protested the war as a wasteful enterprise for the wealthy and powerful from which workingmen would gain nothing. American socialists drew ammunition from the fact that this was a foreign war in which the United States did not have a direct stake. Along with other groups, they urged Americans to refuse to fight, leading to government persecution of many anti-war groups during the period. A "red scare" orchestrated by Attorney General A. Mitchell Palmer and the young J. Edgar Hoover in the mid-1910s led to massive arrests and deportations of leading Leftists and Socialists.

Coupled with the growth of the middle class and conspicuous consumption in the 1920s, police repression helped finally to slow the growth of socialism for more than a decade. By 1922, only 15,000 people belonged to the Socialist Party. Socialism would rise again in later decades, but it never regained the height of popularity it enjoyed during the early 20th century.

"THESE ARE THE TIMES THAT TRY MEN'S SOULS" This well-known phrase opened Thomas Paine's series of papers *The American Crisis* in 1776. The papers supported the American Revolution and appeared throughout the Revolutionary War. Author of the highly influential pamphlet *Common Sense*, Paine hoped *The American Crisis* would lift the morale of George Washington's men fighting in the Continental Army. The opening line is still used today during times of conflict or trouble, as evidenced by Charles Schenck's use of it in his pamphlet.

Biographies and Organizations
Words, War, and the Workplace

Library of Congress

ADAMS, JOHN

John Adams was born on October 30, 1735, in Braintree (now Quincy), Massachusetts. He graduated from Harvard College in 1755, was admitted to the bar in 1758, and quickly established a successful Boston practice. In 1774, he was chosen as one of the delegates from Massachusetts to the First Continental Congress. At the Second Continental Congress in 1775, Adams pressed for a complete break with England. In 1778, he was sent to Europe, where he served as an American minister until 1788. After his return, he was elected the first vice president of the United States, a post to which he was reelected in 1792. In 1796, Adams won a narrow victory for the presidency. His administration was dominated by the growth of the two-party system and the repercussions of the French Revolution. Adams retired to Braintree after leaving the White House in 1801. He died on July 4, 1826.

Between 1798 and 1800, an undeclared naval war, known as the Quasi-War, raged between the United States and France. The outbreak of hostilities enabled the Federalist Party to push the repressive Alien and Sedition Acts through Congress. The Acts were aimed against the many foreign-born (especially French and Irish) critics of the government and made it more difficult for them to become American citizens. The Acts also allowed the government to prosecute citizens who expressed opposition to its policies. Eleven men, mostly newspaper editors, were convicted for their opinions. Although no one was deported, immigration was discouraged, and some foreigners left the country.

President Adams saw the acts as wartime measures, intended to protect the new nation from enemy agents operating within the United States. The true intent, however, was to stifle the anti-Federalist press. Adams did not support the Acts, but he also did not oppose them. His signing of the Alien and Sedition Acts were characterized by historians as one of "the most reprehensible acts of his presidency." His wife Abigail was open in her support of the Sedition Act, which she felt would end the "wicked and base, violent and culminating abuse" of the press. The laws were vigorously opposed by Vice President Thomas Jefferson and his Democratic-Republican Party, who felt the acts violated the First Amendment's guarantee of free speech.

Without the support of many of the Federalists and vilified by the Democratic-Republicans for not vetoing the Alien and Sedition Acts, Adams was defeated by Jefferson in the election of 1800. Interestingly, the election was the first to feature an active propaganda campaign, financed by Jefferson. In a series of essays in the *Richmond Examiner,* Adams was called "a repulsive pedant," a "gross hypocrite," and an "egregious fool" by propagandist James Callender. The Sedition Act made it a crime to openly criticize the president, and Callender was found guilty and sent to jail.

AMERICAN SOCIALIST PARTY

Members of a variety of left-wing movements united with the Social Democratic Party to form the Socialist Party of America (SPA) around the turn of the 20th century. The SPA achieved its peak strength in the 1912 elections when its candidate for U.S. president, Eugene V. Debs, won six percent of the popular vote.

Socialism never had the appeal in the United States that it had in Europe. After World War I, when the Socialists maintained an unpopular anti-war position, the Party's strength declined dramatically. This weakening was exacerbated by a schism among SPA members in 1919 that led to the formation of the Communist Party.

Biographies and Organizations
Words, War, and the Workplace, cont.

BRANDEIS, LOUIS

Louis Brandeis was born in Kentucky in 1856 to Jewish parents who had immigrated from Bohemia. He graduated from Harvard Law School in 1877 and established a successful law practice in Boston. Brandeis became well known as an articulate liberal advocate. Nicknamed the "People's Attorney," he frequently donated his legal services on behalf of a great variety of worthy causes. In 1916, Brandeis was nominated to the Supreme Court. Along with his colleague Oliver Wendell Holmes, he became famous for his dissenting opinions in support of liberal causes. Brandeis devoted his energy both before and after his retirement from the Court in 1939 to the Zionist movement. He died in 1941.

Brandeis was a proponent of judicial activism and supported legislation created "to remold . . . economic practices and institutions to meet changing social and economic needs" (*New State Ice Cream Co. v. Liebmann,* 1931). He opposed government actions that inhibited freedom of speech, freedom of assembly, freedom of the press, and freedom of religion. Although he wrote relatively few dissents (44 out of 528 decisions), his opinions were very significant because they frequently provided the basis upon which the law would be reinterpreted by a more liberal and activist Supreme Court in future decades.

DEBS, EUGENE V.

Library of Congress

E ugene V. Debs was born in 1855 in Terre Haute, Indiana, to immigrant parents from France. Largely self-educated, he left school at age fifteen to work as a locomotive fireman. He served in the state legislature as a Democrat and then concentrated on building unions of workmen to advocate better working conditions and employee rights. By 1893, he had organized the American Railway Union, the nation's first industrial union. He later helped found the Industrial Workers of the World (IWW). Debs turned to Socialism as a result of the severe depression of the 1890s and what he saw as the increasing use of government power against the rights of labor. He was the presidential candidate of the Social Democratic Party in 1900 and the candidate of the Socialist Party of America in 1904, 1908, 1912, and 1920. He spent his last years editing the Socialist weekly *American Appeal* and writing a book about the need to improve prison conditions. Debs died in 1926.

When the Socialist Party refused to support the participation of the United States in World War I, Debs at first maintained a low anti-war profile. But in 1918, angered by the government's arrest of political radicals for sedition, he delivered a harsh speech in Canton, Ohio, attacking the administration of President Woodrow Wilson for its unconstitutional use of the Espionage and Sedition Acts to imprison radicals. Debs himself was then indicted under the Espionage Act for sedition on two counts: for attempting to "cause and incite insubordination, disloyalty, mutiny and refusal of duty in the military and naval forces of the United States" and for obstructing military recruiting and enlisting. He was tried and sentenced to serve two concurrent ten-year terms in federal prison. The U.S. Supreme Court heard his appeal and ruled unanimously in 1919 that since the nation was at war, issues of national security were more important than those of individual rights under the Constitution. His conviction upheld, Debs ran for president in 1920 while an inmate at the Atlanta federal penitentiary.

Biographies and Organizations
Words, War, and the Workplace, cont.

UPI-Bettmann/Corbis

GITLOW, BENJAMIN

Benjamin Gitlow was born in Elizabethport, New Jersey, in 1891, the son of Russian-Jewish immigrants. Growing up in poverty in New York City, he became interested in Socialism and joined the Socialist Party in 1909. He quickly rose through the Party ranks and was elected to the New York Assembly. The Russian Revolution of 1917 turned him from Socialism, however, and Gitlow helped form the Communist Labor Party in 1919. He is considered the founder of the American Communist Party. Gitlow was active in the Communist movement throughout the 1920s, running for vice president of the United States in 1924 and 1928. Factions in the movement in the 1930s disenchanted him, however, and by the end of the decade, he had denounced Communism completely. He died in 1965.

Gitlow was the business manager of the communist newspaper *Revolutionary Age*. In 1919, he and three others were indicted for advocating Communism and violating New York's Criminal Anarchy Act. Represented by famous attorney Clarence Darrow, he spoke on the stand in his own defense and proclaimed that capitalism "has brought untold misery and hardships to the working man." Gitlow was found guilty in 1920 and sentenced to five to ten years' hard labor. His co-defendants were eventually pardoned, but Gitlow was taken on by the American Civil Liberties Union (ACLU) as a test case of the New York law. The U.S. Supreme Court ruled on *Gitlow v. New York* in June, 1925 and upheld his conviction. Justices Oliver Wendell Holmes and Louis Brandeis famously dissented. Having been released pending his appeal, Gitlow returned to prison. He was pardoned by New York's governor on December 11, 1925.

GOLDMAN, EMMA

Emma Goldman was born in Russia in 1869. In 1885, she decided to emigrate to the United States rather than submit to an arranged marriage. In the United States, she obtained work in clothing factories. She found working conditions oppressive and became a public critic of capitalism. In 1889, Goldman moved to New York City, where she joined the anarchist movement. She was imprisoned in 1893 for delivering an inflammatory speech to unemployed men in New York's Union Square. Upon her release, she lectured in the United States and Europe. She joined the anti-Fascists in Spain during the Spanish Civil War and was organizing on their behalf in Canada when she died in Toronto in May, 1940.

Library of Congress

As an anarchist writer, lecturer, and agitator, Goldman was one of the most outstanding rebels in American history. She was an advocate of birth control, women's rights, free speech, and sexual liberation. For speaking out in favor of birth control in 1916, she spent time in jail. In 1917, Goldman was sentenced to two years in prison for helping men resist the draft for World War I. She was released in 1919, immediately declared a subversive alien, and deported to Russia with more than 200 other radicals. According to FBI director J. Edgar Hoover, deporting Goldman was one of his finest achievements.

Biographies and Organizations
Words, War, and the Workplace, cont.

Library of Congress

HOLMES, OLIVER WENDELL

Oliver Wendell Holmes was born in Boston, Massachusetts, in 1841. After serving in the Union Army during the Civil War, he attended Harvard Law School. A brilliant legal mind, Holmes was appointed to the State Supreme Court of Massachusetts. In 1902, President Theodore Roosevelt appointed him to the U.S. Supreme Court, where he served for 30 years. Holmes died in 1935.

As a jurist, Holmes was nicknamed "The Great Dissenter" since he often disagreed with his Court colleagues on such issues as government interference in business. But it was as an advocate of free speech that Holmes made his mark. In two important cases, *Abrams v. United States* (1919) and *Gitlow v. New York* (1925), Holmes affirmed that Americans could publish material critical of the government provided that it was not in danger of bringing about its immediate, possibly violent, downfall.

Library of Congress

MASON, GEORGE

George Mason was born into a prominent family in Fairfax County, Virginia, in 1725. He replaced George Washington in the Virginia House of Burgesses in 1775. The following year, he wrote the Virginia Declaration of Rights and most of Virginia's new state constitution. The Declaration of Rights became a model for the other colonies and influenced the writing of the Declaration of Independence and the Bill of Rights. Mason played a central role in the debates at the Constitutional Convention but could not bring himself to sign the document (and fought against ratification in the Virginia Convention in 1788) because of the lack of a Bill of Rights and the continuation of slavery. He died in 1792.

Adopted by the Virginia Convention on June 12, 1776, the Virginia Declaration of Rights foreshadowed the Declaration of Independence with its championship of individual liberty in the early days of the American Revolution. Articles XII and XVI especially influenced the Bill of Rights. Mason wrote in Article XII that "the freedom of the press is one of the greatest bulwarks of liberty and can never be restrained but by despotic governments," while Article XVI says "all men are equally entitled to the free exercise of religion."

SCHENCK, CHARLES

Charles Schenck was the self-proclaimed general secretary of the American Socialist Party who urged potential draftees to refuse to fight in World War I. For this act, he was prosecuted under the Espionage Act of 1917. The case reached the Supreme Court in 1919, and his conviction was upheld.

U.S. SUPREME COURT

The U.S. Supreme Court is the highest authority in the judicial branch. It was created by the Judiciary Act of 1789, under the provisions of the Constitution. It has jurisdiction over cases relating to the Constitution, federal laws, and treaties involving the United States. The Court consists of a chief justice and eight associate justices. Any decision requires the participation of at least six justices. Decisions are determined by a simple majority and are handed down with an opinion written by one of the justices in the majority. Justices disagreeing with the majority opinion may write dissenting opinions, and justices agreeing with the outcome but disagreeing with the logic of the majority may write concurring opinions. Supreme Court justices have made a lasting impact on American history, helping to ensure that the Constitution is adapted to changing times and circumstances.

Court Cases, Amendments, and Acts
Words, War, and the Workplace

ABRAMS v. UNITED STATES (1919)

Following on the heels of the Supreme Court's ruling in *Debs v. United States* (1919), *Abrams v. United States* reinforced the Court's earlier stance on the Espionage Act of 1917 and the Sedition Act of 1918 and the relative weight of individual liberty versus national security during times of war and national crisis. Unlike *Debs*, the decision in *Abrams* was not unanimous, with two justices dissenting on the grounds that the Court must uphold stricter standards for the "clear and present danger" test.

ALIEN AND SEDITION ACTS OF 1798

Though they were committed to freedom, the American founders often differed as to how freedom should be applied to specific controversies, as shown by the Alien and Sedition Acts. The four bills were pushed through the U.S. Congress by the Federalists in 1798 in an attempt to silence their critics, led by Thomas Jefferson and the Democratic-Republican Party. The Alien and Sedition Acts made it more difficult for aliens to become U.S. citizens, gave the president the power to deport aliens in the event of war, and gave the government the power to prosecute citizens who wrote or published works that were critical of the government, Congress, or the president.

Of the four laws that make up the Act's, the Sedition Act was the most controversial. This law, which appears to violate the First Amendment, made it a crime to publish "any false, scandalous, and malicious" criticism of the government, the Congress, or the president. Altogether, eleven individuals, all Democratic-Republicans, were convicted under this law. The law was set to expire just before the inauguration of the new president (Jefferson), but he exercised his authority to release those who were still in jail and dismiss all pending prosecutions.

BILL OF RIGHTS

The first ten amendments to the U.S. Constitution, the Bill of Rights was ratified by the requisite number of states on December 15, 1791, and went into effect on March 1, 1792. The U.S. House of Representatives had already granted its approval for the amendments on September 24, 1789, with the U.S. Senate concurring on the following day. The Bill of Rights assuaged the fears of many anti-federalists, those who were concerned that the newly adopted federal Constitution concentrated too much power in the national government, and feared that the new government might deprive the people of certain fundamental liberties. Although the Bill of Rights was originally intended to apply only to the national government, beginning in the late 19th century, the U.S. Supreme Court mandated that many of the liberties protected by the various amendments to the Constitution must be acknowledged by state governments as well.

BRANDENBURG v. OHIO (1969)

Brandenburg v. Ohio effectively overturned the Supreme Court's decision in *California v. Whitney* (1927) by declaring Ohio's criminal syndicalism law to be invalid. The defendant was a member of the Ku Klux Klan who had been filmed at an isolated cross-burning rally uttering racial slurs and speaking of the need for "revengeance." The Court said that *Dennis v. United States* (1951) and other decisions established the principle that a state could not condemn the advocacy of either force or disobedience to law, except where such advocacy was directed to incite imminent lawless action and was likely to produce such action.

Justice Hugo Black and Justice William O. Douglas' concurring opinions indicated their continuing rejection of the "clear and present danger" test. Douglas indicated that he would limit prosecutions to cases where speech is "brigaded with action," like Holmes' classic example in *Schenck v. United States* (1919) of falsely shouting "fire!" in a crowded theater. *Brandenburg* reflects the Supreme Court's current expansive view of freedom of speech.

Court Cases, Amendments, and Acts
Words, War, and the Workplace, cont.

CONSCRIPTION ACT (1917)

On May 18, 1917, Congress approved the "Proclamation Establishing Conscription," also known as the Conscription Act. Under this act, all American men between twenty-one and thirty years old had to register with the government so that they could be drawn into the military if necessary.

DENNIS v. UNITED STATES (1951)

In *Dennis v. United States*, the Supreme Court upheld the conviction of Eugene Dennis and ten other leaders of the American Communist Party. The group had been indicted under the Smith Act for advocating the violent overthrow of the government and for organizing a political party for that purpose.

Chief Justice Fred Vinson cited the "clear and present danger" test in his decision, but it arguably shared greater affinity with *Gitlow v. New York* (1925) than *Schenck v. United States* (1919). Vinson observed that the "clear and present danger" test "cannot mean that before the Government may act, it must wait until the putsch [a secret plot to overthrow the government] is about to be executed, the plans have been laid and the signal is awaited." Vinson thus adopted a reformulation of the "clear and present danger" test known as the "gravity of evil" test. This test has been developed by U.S. appellate judge Learned Hand who said "In each case [courts] must ask whether the gravity of the 'evil,' discounted by its improbability, justifies such invasion of free speech as is necessary to avoid the danger."

In his dissent, Justice William O. Douglas argued that free speech was absolute: it was the rule, not the exception. He did not find sufficient evidence in the record that the American Communists posed a clear and present danger to the nation, and he expressed his faith that the American people would reject Communist ideology.

ESPIONAGE ACT OF 1917

The Espionage Act of 1917 was the first act directed against espionage and treason adopted by Congress since the Alien and Sedition Acts of 1798. The original bill contained provisions against both espionage and criticism of the government, but the latter provisions were deleted after free speech concerns were raised in Congress. The Espionage Act was followed by the Sedition Act in 1918. Both acts were repealed in 1921.

FIRST AMENDMENT OF THE UNITED STATES CONSTITUTION

The most cherished and cited of all constitutional amendments, the First Amendment protects freedom of religion, speech, press, peaceable assembly, and petition. Although it was originally the third of twelve proposed amendments (the first two of which were not initially ratified), there is some rightful symbolism in the fact that this important amendment now heads the Bill of Rights.

Court Cases, Amendments, and Acts
Words, War, and the Workplace, cont.

GITLOW v. NEW YORK (1925)

Gitlow v. New York, a seven-to-two decision for the Supreme Court written by Justice Edward Sanford, upheld the conviction of Benjamin Gitlow and three other socialists who had violated New York's Criminal Anarchy Law. The law sought to punish those who advocated the overthrow of the government, and Gitlow had published a revolutionary pamphlet entitled "The Left Wing Manifesto" that seemed to do just that.

In the decision, Sanford argued that the freedom of speech did not apply to words designed to bring about the overthrow of the government. He then articulated what is often called the "bad tendency" test: "A single revolutionary spark may kindle a fire. . . . It cannot be said that the State is acting arbitrarily or unreasonably when . . . to protect the public peace and safety, it seeks to extinguish the spark without waiting until it has enkindled the flame or blazed into the conflagration."

Justice Oliver Wendell Holmes dissented and was joined by Justice Louis Brandeis. After applying the "clear and present danger" test that he had developed in *Schenck v. United States*, Holmes did not believe that Gitlow's publications posed such a danger. He further observed, "If in the long run the beliefs expressed in proletarian dictatorship are destined to be accepted by the dominant forces of the community, the only meaning of free speech is that they should be given a chance and have their way."

NINTH AMENDMENT

One of the most elusive and controversial amendments to the Constitution is the Ninth Amendment. Ratified in 1791 as part of the Bill of Rights, it maintains that the rights enumerated in the Bill of Rights are not the only ones held by the people. One of the Federalists' original objections to the inclusion of a bill of rights was that it would be impossible to make a complete list of human rights. Such a bill might prove dangerous if observers concluded that because a right was not enumerated it had therefore been forfeited. The Ninth Amendment appears to have been introduced with this problem in mind.

SCHENCK v. UNITED STATES (1919)

This Supreme Court case took shape when an American socialist, Charles Schenck, was prosecuted for sedition under the Espionage Act of 1917. He had sent 15,000 anti-war pamphlets through the mail to potential draftees. Schenck urged the men to refuse to fight when the United States was entering World War I and preparing to send troops overseas. Although the language was fiery, the pamphlet did not advocate violent resistance. Yet the Espionage Act had criminalized actions that aided America's enemies. Anyone who tried to deprive the United States of soldiers was technically helping the enemy. By labeling protest an act of treason, the Espionage Act set an individual's right to speak freely against the nation's right to look after its own interests. The *Schenck* case was about deciding which right took precedence.

Two important concepts arose from the Supreme Court's unanimous decision in *Schenck v. United States*. As written by Justice Oliver Wendell Holmes, they are central to understanding the course of free speech legislation in the modern United States.

1. "falsely shouting fire in a theater and causing a panic": Holmes' famous and oft-quoted analogy from this opinion stated that free speech was not absolute, but rather had to be looked at within its context.

2. "clear and present danger" test: taking its cue from the "shouting fire" idea, this test dictates that freedom of speech should be restricted only in cases where such speech constitutes a "clear and present danger" that Congress has a right to address.

Court Cases, Amendments, and Acts
Words, War, and the Workplace, cont.

SEDITION ACT OF 1918

Enacted on May 16, 1918, the Sedition Act amended the Espionage Act of 1917, mandating stricter punishments for those who attempted to undermine the U.S. war effort during World War I. It put strict limits on speaking, writing, printing, and publishing about the U.S. government, the U.S. Constitution, the U.S. military, and the U.S. flag during wartime. "Whoever shall by word or act support or favor the cause of any country with which the United States is at war or by word or act oppose the cause of the United States therein, shall be punished by a fine of not more than $10,000 or the imprisonment for not more than twenty years, or both," it read. The Sedition Act was intended primarily to curb the activities of Socialists and Pacifists. In 1919, it was used along with the Espionage Act of 1917 to prosecute Socialist Party leader Eugene V. Debs.

Acting on the initiative provided by the 1918 legislation, Attorney General A. Mitchell Palmer initiated the notorious "Palmer raids." More than 5,000 activists were arrested for deportation over a three-month period. Federal agents invaded homes, schools, churches, and other buildings to seize militants in an attempt to halt their labor-organizing efforts. On one night alone, in January of 1920, more than 2,500 arrests were made in thirty-one cities across the country. Citizens as well as non-citizens were apprehended and released only on proof of citizenship or legal residence in the United States.

SMITH ACT (1940)

Also known as the Alien Registration Act, the Smith Act (it was sponsored by Representative Howard Smith of Virginia) was adopted on June 29, 1940. This took place prior to American entry into World War II but against the backdrop of world war and fears of domestic subversion. The law made it illegal to "advocate, abet, advise, or teach" the violent overthrow of the government or to organize or conspire to organize a party for this purpose.

Most prosecutions under the Smith Act were directed at members of the American Communist Party. Top leaders of the Party were jailed in convictions that were upheld in *Dennis v. United States* (1951) under the so-called modification of the "clear and present danger" test known as the "gravity of the evil" test. However, in *Yates v. United States* (1957) and *Scales v. United States* (1961), the Supreme Court read the Smith Act more restrictively. Of 141 persons indicted under the law, only twenty-nine served jail time.

THIRTEENTH AMENDMENT

The Thirteenth Amendment was added to the Constitution in the last days of the Civil War. Its sole purpose was to outlaw African American slavery permanently within the United States.

UNITED STATES CONSTITUTION

The "supreme law of the land," the U.S. Constitution was drafted by legislators in Philadelphia, Pennsylvania, between July and September 1787. The delegates had originally met to revise the Articles of Confederation, the first document used to frame the U.S. government, but decided instead to discard the Articles and create an entirely new form of government. The delegates worked to achieve a delicate balance by establishing a government powerful enough to be effective but not oppressive. The resulting document establishes the country's

Court Cases, Amendments, and Acts
Words, War, and the Workplace, cont.

republican principles, outlines the checks and balances between the three branches of government, and suggests the federalist relationship between the national and state governments. After New Hampshire ratified the document on June 21, 1788, the new form of government had the necessary support of three-fourths of the states to go into effect, which it did on July 2 of that year. The U.S. Constitution has remained firmly at the center of American government ever since.

WHITNEY v. CALIFORNIA (1927)

In *Whitney v. California,* the Supreme Court upheld the conviction of a prominent social activist, Charlotte Anita Whitney, for violating the California Criminal Syndicalism Act. Whitney had joined the Communist Labor Party and attended its convention, even though she opposed the Party's advocacy of violence. Relying heavily on the Court's decision in *Gitlow v. New York* (1925), Justice Edward Sanford upheld the judgment of the California state legislature that organizations advocating violence posed a danger to the state against which it had a right to legislate.

Justice Louis Brandeis' concurring opinion, joined by Justice Oliver Wendell Holmes, reads more like a dissent. Although he ultimately accepted evidence that the Communist Labor Party was engaged in a conspiracy to commit serious crimes that the state had a right to forestall, Brandeis emphasized the value of free speech as both a means and an end. In a statement that has often been cited, Brandeis wrote about the American Founders:

*They believed that freedom to think as you will and to speak as you think
are means indispensable to the discovery and spread of political truth; that
without free speech and assembly discussion would be futile; that with
them, discussion affords ordinarily adequate protection against the dissemi-
nation of noxious doctrine; that public discussion is a political duty; and
that this should be a fundamental principle of the American government.*

Brandenburg v. Ohio overturned *Whitney v. California* in 1969.

YATES *v.* UNITED STATES (1957)

In *Yates v. United States*, the Supreme Court reversed the convictions of
fourteen Communist Party leaders who had been convicted under the
Alien Registration Act (also known as the Smith Act) for conspiracy.
Among other points, the Court decided that the conviction based upon
the act's prohibition against advocacy of overthrowing the government
was unconstitutional, because of the difference between advocacy of
doctrine or belief and advocacy of action. The Court did not directly
hold the Smith Act unconstitutional, but it made convictions under the
act difficult. No further prosecutions occurred.

Justices Hugo Black and William O. Douglas would have acquitted all
the defendants. They argued that prosecutions under the Smith Act
were "more in line with the philosophy of authoritarian government
than with that expressed by our First Amendment." By contrast, Justice
Tom Clark would have confirmed all the convictions. Although the
Communists in *Yates* were in a "lower echelon in the party hierarchy"
than those in *Dennis v. United States*, Clark argued that they "served in
the same army and were engaged in the same mission."

Actions Speak
Louder than
Words

Defining Moment

U.S. Supreme Court

Actions Speak Louder than Words

Texas v. Johnson (1989) was one of the U.S. Supreme Court's most controversial decisions of recent years. The issue that it raises—whether or not American citizens have the right to burn their own national flag in political protest—was first debated in the 1960s and it remains unresolved. *Texas v. Johnson* prompted numerous calls for a constitutional amendment to prohibit flag desecration, one as recently as 2005. To understand why this topic has been debated in the public forum for such a long time, it is necessary to walk through its background.

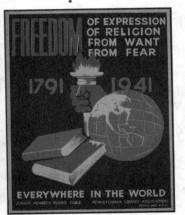

Library of Congress

Poster promoting President Franklin Delano Roosevelt's "four freedoms." In January 1941, Roosevelt spoke of America's duty to spread "four freedoms"—freedom of speech and religion, freedom from want and fear—to the rest of the world. The dates "1791" and "1941" marked the 150th anniversary of the Bill of Rights.

The issue of proper treatment for the American flag emerged during World War II. Congress passed a resolution laying out proper flag etiquette that carried no penalties for noncompliance. In *West Virginia Board of Education v. Barnette* (1943) and *Taylor v. Mississippi* (1943) the Supreme Court ruled that persons could not be forced to salute the flag, and they could not be penalized for encouraging others to refuse to salute either. Despite the fact that America was at war, the government was interested in encouraging patriotic display but not regulating it. However, World War II was a popular war. After the Japanese attack on Pearl Harbor, there was little objection to U.S. involvement. So there was little anti-war political protest to force lawmakers or jurists to take a stronger stance on issues of respect for national symbols.

The atmosphere was radically different during the controversial Vietnam War. In the 1960s, flag desecration emerged as a form of political protest. Anti-war protesters frequently burned U.S. flags or representations of the flag in order to show their outrage at America's role in Vietnam.

A televised incident of flag burning in Central Park in April 1967 precipitated the first federal legislation on the subject. The Flag Protection Act, adopted in 1968, made it illegal to desecrate the flag or show contempt for it in any way. Several state legislatures responded by passing similar laws. The constitutionality of these laws was challenged, and the U.S. Supreme Court eventually struck down several of them. In one case, a teenager had sewn a flag patch to his jeans; in another, a man had taped a peace symbol to a flag. The Court decided each case on particular grounds, basing their decisions on complex legal arguments rather than sweeping constitutional interpretations. But underpinning the Court's rulings was an interpretation of flag desecration as a form of symbolic speech, protected by the First Amendment.

Politically inspired flag desecration became relatively rare after the United States pulled out of Vietnam in the early 1970s, and the Supreme Court issued no further decisions on the subject between 1974 and 1989. During the ensuing fifteen years, the political climate in this country changed. The rampant criticism of the U.S. government gave way to a renewed emphasis on American strength at home and abroad. Recovering from the demoralizing effects of Vietnam, the nation positioned itself as a counterweight to the threat of the mighty Soviet Union. The United States was seen as defending the world from Soviet oppression. Renewed national pride meant renewed importance placed upon respect for national institutions.

Actions Speak Louder than Words, cont.

Time Life Pictures/Getty Images

Gregory Lee Johnson is arrested in front of the city hall in Dallas, Texas, for his flag-burning demonstration during the 1984 Republican National Convention. Johnson was prosecuted under a Texas state law, but the landmark Supreme Court decision Texas v. Johnson *(1989) overturned his conviction. Even so, flag burning remains a contentious free speech issue.*

This was the situation in 1984, when political protester Gregory Lee Johnson burned an American flag outside the Republican National Convention in Dallas, Texas. He burned the flag to protest the renomination of President Ronald Reagan for election that year, as well as the policies of the administration more generally. During the burning, protesters chanted "America, the red, white, and blue, we spit on you." Johnson was arrested for violating a Texas statute that forbid the desecration of a venerated object. He was tried, fined, and sentenced to a year in prison. One Texas court of appeals upheld his conviction, and another struck it down. The case was too divisive to be put to rest easily.

Texas v. Johnson reached the U.S. Supreme Court in 1989. The state of Texas argued that it had passed a law to prohibit flag burning for two reasons: to preserve the flag as a symbol of national unity and to prevent breaches of the peace. However, there was a profound free speech question in play. It becomes clear if it is remembered that, technically, flag burning was not illegal in Texas. Burning was actually a means of disposing of a worn or damaged U.S. flag (an accepted practice and quite legal). So therefore, Texas' law was *specifically* directed against political speech because it *only* punished the act of flag burning when it expresses a political view.

Justice William Brennan led a five-to-four majority affirming that Johnson's conduct was a form of symbolic speech protected by the First and Fourteenth Amendments. Freedom of expression took precedence over either of the arguments put forward by Texas. In addition, Brennan rejected the idea that flag burning constituted a danger to the nation's well-being, and so necessitated a law forbidding it. But Chief Justice William Rehnquist wrote a minority opinion, which categorized the flag as a unique American symbol and entitled to protection not accorded other emblems. He claimed that flag burning was designed to antagonize others, not to express thoughts. Rehnquist said that Johnson's right to express his ideas was not at issue: the protester could say anything he wanted. The objection was only to this one particular means of expressing them.

U.S. Supreme Court
The courtroom in the Supreme Court where cases are heard.

U.S. Supreme Court

As it had divided the Court, flag burning divided public opinion. Many people condemned the activity despite the Court's ruling in *Texas v. Johnson*. Congress rushed to pass the Flag Protection Act of 1989, making it a federal crime to "knowingly mutilate, deface, physically defile, burn, maintain on the floor or ground, or trample upon any flag of the United States." The Act attempted to sidestep the constitutional issue altogether. It made flag abuse illegal in itself, regardless of the political motive of the abuser or the reactions of those who might be offended by it. The law was written to punish conduct—the act of deliberately damaging a flag—rather than speech, symbolic or otherwise.

This argument failed to persuade the U.S. Supreme Court, however, which ruled the Flag Protection Act unconstitutional in the landmark case of *United States v. Eichman* (1990). "Although the Flag Protection Act contains no explicit content-based limitation on the scope of prohibited conduct," wrote Justice William Brennan, writing for the

Actions Speak Louder than Words, cont.

Court majority, "it is . . . clear that the Government's . . . interest is 'related to the suppression of free expression.' Punishing desecration of the flag dilutes the very freedom that makes this emblem so revered, and worth revering." Again, four justices disagreed with the majority. "The flag uniquely symbolizes the ideas of liberty, equality, and tolerance," Justice John Paul Stevens wrote in dissent. Those wishing to express disagreement with government policies have many other means at their disposal, he argued. They did not need the right to desecrate this unique symbol of the nation's "shared ideals."

Because it is so open to interpretation, because the Supreme Court has shown itself to be divided on the issue, and because of its emotional impact, flag desecration will probably remain the most elusive and most persistent free speech issue brought before U.S. courts in the coming years.

Citations

West Virginia Board of Education v. Barnette, 319 US 624 (1943)

Taylor v. Mississippi, 319 US 583 (1943)

United States v. Eichman, 496 US 310 (1990)

Lesson Overview

This lesson will take place in two stages. In Part I, the teacher will provide short excerpts of three Supreme Court free speech rulings between 1968 and 1990 while leading the students in a discussion of the Supreme Court's increasingly more permissive view of free speech across the 20th century.

In Part II, the teacher will lead the students in a full class debate over the case *Texas v. Johnson.* In this incident, Gregory Lee Johnson burned an American flag in protest of President Reagan's war policies and was prosecuted under Texas state law. The students will use their knowledge of the previous Supreme Court free speech rulings as well as of the First Amendment to form their opinions about whether Johnson was acting within the parameters of his civil rights when he burned the flag. Once the debate has been completed, the teacher will reveal the real Supreme Court ruling.

Actions Speak Louder than Words

Authors

CHRIS MULLIN
SANTA YNEZ VALLEY
UNION HIGH SCHOOL

BRETT PIERSMA
SANTA YNEZ VALLEY
UNION HIGH SCHOOL

Lesson Plan Part I
Class Discussion

To begin the first portion of this activity, the teacher should provide the students with a handout of the First Amendment to the Constitution (this document can also be projected as a slide or written out on the board). The teacher should ask a student to volunteer to read the amendment out loud for the class. Once the student has finished reading, the teacher can pose the following questions:

- What specific actions does this amendment protect?
- What is the government prohibited from doing?
- Does it surprise you to see any of these protections included in the 1790s?
- Do you think our citizens enjoy these rights today?
- Is the government ever criticized for violating these rights?
- Do you have absolute freedom of speech? At school? In public?
- What limits do you think you have on your freedom of speech?

Once the teacher has completed the discussion on the First Amendment and free speech, he or she should pass out the excerpts from the *O'Brien* and *Brandenburg* cases and ask a student to read them aloud.

Activity
LESSON PLAN PART I

For this portion of the activity, students will need copies of:

- Excerpt from the First Amendment to the Constitution, p. 75
- Excerpt from *United States v. O'Brien* (1968), p. 76
- Excerpt from *Brandenburg v. Ohio* (1969), p. 77

Once the students are done, the teacher should direct the discussion using the following prompts:

- Does the government have a legitimate argument for preventing the burning of draft cards?
- How might the constitutional power of Congress to "raise and support armies" be used against O'Brien?
- What kinds of activities do you believe would incite "imminent lawless activities" among citizens?
- Is it justified to ban these types of activities?
- Should a government be able to limit symbolic speech if that speech is offensive to others?
- How is burning a draft card similar to or different from burning an American flag?
- Based on these court rulings (and *Schenck* if students have completed the first Activity), has free speech become more or less controlled in recent years?

Lesson Plan Part II
The Class Debate

Now that the students have focused on both the First Amendment and some critical Supreme Court cases of the 20th century, they are ready to take part in a full class debate on the issue of flag burning.

Using either a data projector or writing on the whiteboard, the teacher will present a series of statements, one at a time, relating to the *Texas v. Johnson* case (see below). Then the teacher will write the words: "I agree" with an arrow pointing to the right and "I disagree" with an arrow pointing to the left. The teacher will then invite the students to get up from their desks and stand on the side of the room that corresponds to their opinion on each statement. Students who are unsure of their position can remain standing in the middle of the room and move one way or the other if they are convinced by one side or the other. Once the students have taken their position, the teacher should facilitate an informal debate between the students on each statement:

- The American flag is a sacred symbol of our nation that should be protected.
- Our First Amendment rights are more important than any symbol such as a flag.
- People should be allowed to burn the American flag as long as they do not break any laws.
- Burning an American flag is an activity directed toward inciting lawless action.
- The State of Texas violated Gregory Lee Johnson's rights when it arrested him.

After each division, the teacher should encourage a variety of voices and steer the discussion toward the question of constitutionality. The teacher should also try to get the students to justify their opinions by citing either the First Amendment or the ensuing Supreme Court rulings. Students may wish to voice their dislike of Johnson's message, but the teacher should try to focus the debate on the question of legality rather than on popularity.

Activity
LESSON PLAN PART II

For this portion of the activity, students will need copies of:

- Excerpt from the First Amendment to the Constitution, p. 75
- Excerpt from *United States v. O'Brien* (1968), p. 76
- Excerpt from *Texas v. Johnson* (1989), p. 78
- OpEd 1: *The Dallas Morning News,* July 23, 1989, p. 79
- OpEd 2: *The New York Times,* July 19, 1989, p. 81
- Article: *The Dallas Morning News,* October 31, 1989, p. 83

Once all questions have been posed and the debates conducted, students should return to their seats. The teacher then should distribute the excerpt from the Supreme Court's ruling *Texas v. Johnson* in which Johnson's conviction was overturned. Discuss the implications of this ruling using the following prompts:

• What do you think Justice Brennan (author of the decision) means by "a principal function of free speech under our system of government is to invite dispute"?
• Do you agree that even though an idea is offensive, it should be protected?
• What are some actions and ideas today that are offensive? Should they be protected?

EXTENSION WRITING ASSIGNMENT: LETTERS TO THE EDITOR
Once students have explored the issues surrounding flag burning and free speech, they can now take part in this follow-up assignment, which will provide them with the chance to express their thoughts and opinions in writing. Pass out copies of OpEd1, OpEd2, and the Article. Explain to the students that they will be reading both a factual account of the event in question and two editorial responses that express the strong opinions of the writers. Students are to take home and read all three. Once the students have completed their reading, they are to select one of the two editorials and compose a 200-word letter to the editor in reply. In their letter, they should address specific elements of the editorial they have chosen and take a position in favor or against those arguments. The teacher might have to explain the format for letters to the editor and the voice one might expect to hear. In addition, the teacher should explain that students should write their letters from the viewpoint of someone who is living through these events.

Primary Sources

Actions Speak
Louder than
Words

Excerpt
from the First Amendment to the Constitution

Congress shall make no law respecting an establishment of religion, or prohibiting the free exercise thereof; or abridging the freedom of speech, or of the press; or the right of the people peaceably to assemble, and to petition the Government for a redress of grievances.

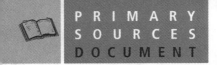

Excerpt
from *United States v. O'Brien* (1968)

We cannot accept the view that an apparently limitless variety of conduct can be labeled 'speech' whenever the person engaging in the conduct intends thereby to express an idea.

We think it clear that a government regulation is sufficiently justified if it is within the constitutional power of the Government; if it furthers an important or substantial governmental interest; if the governmental interest is unrelated to the suppression of free expression; and if the incidental restriction on alleged First Amendment freedoms is no greater than is essential to the furtherance of that interest. We find that the . . . Universal Military Training and Service Act meets all of these requirements, and consequently that O'Brien can be constitutionally convicted for violating it.

Congress has a legitimate and substantial interest in preventing [the] wanton and unrestrained destruction [of Selective Service certificates] and assuring their continuing availability by punishing people who knowingly and willfully destroy or mutilate them.

We think it also apparent that the Nation has a vital interest in having a system for raising armies that functions with maximum efficiency and is capable of easily and quickly responding to continually changing circumstances.

Excerpt
from *Brandenburg v. Ohio* (1969)

These later decisions have fashioned the principle that the constitutional guarantees of free speech and free press do not permit a State to forbid or proscribe advocacy of the use of force or of law violation except where such advocacy is directed to inciting or producing *imminent lawless action* and is likely to incite or produce such action" . . . "the mere abstract teaching . . . of the moral propriety or even moral necessity for a resort to force and violence is not the same as preparing a group for violent action and steeling it to such action." A statute which fails to draw this distinction impermissibly intrudes upon the freedoms guaranteed by the First and Fourteenth Amendments. It sweeps within its condemnation speech which our Constitution has immunized from governmental control . . .

Excerpt
from *Texas v. Johnson* (1989)

The State's position, therefore, amounts to a claim that an audience that takes serious offense at particular expression is necessarily likely to disturb the peace and that the expression may be prohibited on this basis. Our precedents do not countenance such a presumption. On the contrary, they recognize that a principal function of free speech under our system of government is to invite dispute. It may indeed best serve its high purpose when it induces a condition of unrest, creates dissatisfaction with conditions as they are, or even stirs people to anger . . . If there is a bedrock principle underlying the First Amendment, it is that the government may not prohibit the expression of an idea simply because society finds the idea itself offensive or disagreeable.

OpEd 1
The Dallas Morning News, June 23, 1989

EDITORIAL DESK
FLAG BURNING: IT MAY BE LEGAL, BUT IT STILL IS DESPICABLE

What occurred in front of the Dallas City Hall one day during the 1984 Republican Convention should have disgusted any American who holds this country dear. With 100 demonstrators looking on, Gregory Lee Johnson, a member of the Revolutionary Communist Youth Brigade, unfurled an American flag, doused it with kerosene and set it on fire.

Old Glory burned as any piece of cloth would, but to think of the flag in those emotionless terms would be much like thinking of a human being as little more than a container of chemicals. No, the flag is not just a piece of cloth. It is the most powerful symbol we have of our nationhood and of all the principles that make us Americans. Old Glory has been with us since our founding. At the dawn of the American Revolution, it served to unify the 13 colonies. Later, as the young nation matured, it helped win worldwide recognition of our sovereignty. During our lifetime, Old Glory has fluttered over many foreign battlefields as thousands of our brave countrymen have died for the American cause.

Why then, many Americans ask, has the U.S. Supreme Court decided that what Gregory Johnson did was legal? Justice Anthony Kennedy probably best explained the court's thinking: "The hard fact is that sometimes we must make decisions we do not like. We make them because they are right, right in the sense that the law and the Constitution, as we see them, compel the result."

OpEd 1
The Dallas Morning News, June 23, 1989, cont.

A majority of the justices—an unusual alignment of the court's most conservative members and its most liberal—justified the decision by saying, "If there is a bedrock principle underlying the First Amendment, it is that the government may not prohibit the expression of an idea simply because society finds the idea itself offensive or disagreeable."

It is difficult to dispute the justices' argument. When Americans pay respect to the flag, and fight for it, they also are paying homage to, and defending, the fundamental principles it represents, one of which is the freedom of expression. As Justice Kennedy noted, it is one of our nation's great ironies that the flag protects those who hold it in contempt.

What Gregory Lee Johnson did may be legal, but it still is despicable. And while five justices may have reaffirmed the man's right to engage in such extreme protest, that should not be taken to mean they were encouraging others to do so. To the contrary, the court said, the best way Americans could counter a flag-burner's message would be to salute Old Glory themselves.

Copyright 1989 The Dallas Morning News Company

OpEd 2
The New York Times, July 19, 1989

EDITORIAL DESK
HOW TO HONOR THE FLAG

With wiser, braver leadership, Americans would by now be celebrating the Supreme Court's flag-burning decision. The inspiring message would have sunk in: even if some tinhorn thinks he can attract attention by torching one flag in Dallas, all the others wave more gloriously as symbols of liberty and reason.

Instead, Congress is racing to reverse the Court decision. Riding a tide of outraged patriotism, members proclaim that the flag needs to be protected by a constitutional amendment all its own. Even the President of the United States, occupant of the bully pulpit, stoops to exploit the Court decision, just as he exploited a quarrel over the Pledge of Allegiance in last year's campaign.

A leader concerned for the Constitution might be eager to make clear that not one Supreme Court justice approves of setting the flag on fire, while all recognize that doing so is symbolic expression.

Such a leader would hail the strengths of a constitutional democracy in which even this contemptible symbolism is, in a nonviolent political demonstration, protected by the First Amendment.

And such a leader would recognize that, though the outrage felt by many citizens deserves attention, the Constitution deserves respect. It ought not to be amended quickly or lightly — and not at all if a new law can do the job instead.

Without such leadership, courage must come from other quarters. Representative Don Edwards of California offers one example. He strongly opposes amending the Bill of Rights. That unprecedented step would itself be a symbol, he argues — of an America so lacking faith in itself that it endows Gregory Johnson, the Texas flag-burner, with the

power to lessen the flag's meaning for all Americans. The cleanest course would be for Mr. Edwards to delay action on a constitutional amendment by his subcommittee until passions cool.

But that may not be possible. Senate leaders already have agreed to vote by this fall on both an amendment and a flag bill like one offered by Joseph Biden, chairman of the Senate Judiciary Committee. Like Gov. Mario Cuomo of New York, Senator Biden argues that a new statute could protect the flag from desecration without having to invade the Constitution.

Advocates contend that a new statute could be written to avoid the offending part of the Texas law struck down by the Court; it defined desecration as mistreatment of a flag knowing that it will "seriously offend" others. The new approach would make flag mistreatment illegal whether done publicly or privately and say nothing about giving offense. That leaves open the question of whether Congress could prevent defendants from raising the same First Amendment defenses as now.

There's a more promising approach: a statute of the kind suggested by Prof. Burt Neuborne in a letter published today, that punishes harming a flag in a setting where such harm is likely to provoke imminent lawless action. The Supreme Court has, over decades, developed standards for that. Such a law would reassert that flag-burning, like other expressive conduct, can lose its constitutional protection and become prohibited — like "fighting words" — when it incites breaches of the peace.

That kind of law would honor the flag and respect ordinary patriotism while averting the present nervous rush to mark up the Constitution. Contemptuous demonstrators would know that breach-of-the-peace laws still apply. Confident citizens would know that for each flag burned in anger, thousands fly in freedom.

Article
The Dallas Morning News, October 31, 1989

4 BURN FLAGS AT CAPITOL
LANDMARK CASE FIGURE AMONG THOSE ARRESTED
Richard Whittle
Washington Bureau of The *Dallas Morning News*

WASHINGTON — The man who won a U.S. Supreme Court ruling voiding a Texas law that barred flag-burning was arrested with three others Monday after they torched three U.S. flags on the Capitol steps to defy a new federal ban on flag desecration.

Shouting, "Burn, baby, burn," Gregory Lee Johnson, 33, and three others identified as members of the Emergency Committee Against the Flag Amendment and Laws tore apart one flag and set fire to three others before a crowd of photographers, television cameras and Capitol police. "We defy your law," declared Nancy Kent, a spokesman for the protesters, reading a prepared statement. "We challenge you. Arrest us. Test your statute. Take it back to the Supreme Court and try once again to claim it is all consistent with your constitutional standards of free speech."

Capitol police arrested Mr. Johnson and the three other flag burners and charged each with violating the 2-day-old Flag Protection Act of 1989 and with disorderly conduct and demonstrating without a permit under the laws of the District of Columbia.

President Bush allowed the flag protection statute to become law without his signature at midnight Friday because he prefers a constitutional amendment against flag desecration. The new law carries a penalty of up to one year in prison and a $1,000 fine.

District of Columbia law calls for up to 90 days in jail and a $250 fine for disorderly conduct and up to 90 days in jail and a $300 fine for demonstrating without a permit, Capitol police spokesman Dan Nichols said.

Article
The Dallas Morning News, October 31, 1989, cont.

Mr. Nichols identified the people arrested with Mr. Johnson, whose home address was listed as Richmond, Ind., as David Blalock, 39, of Johnstown, Pa.; Shawn Eichman, 24, of New York City; and Scott Tyler, 24, of Chicago.

The four were to be held overnight in the Metropolitan Central Cell Block in Washington for arraignment Tuesday in a federal or District of Columbia court, he said.

Mr. Nichols confirmed that Mr. Johnson was the man whose burning of a U.S. flag during the 1984 Republican National Convention in Dallas led to the Supreme Court ruling that flag-burning was a protected exercise of free speech.

The decision sparked demands for a constitutional amendment to protect the flag and prompted Congress to pass the new flag law. The Senate defeated a proposed constitutional amendment, but supporters contend that without it, the new law may be ruled unconstitutional, as the Texas statute was.

Mr. Nichols could provide no further information about those arrested and said none of the four would be available for comment until after arraignment.

Maria Lyons, who answered a New York telephone number on a press release issued by the Emergency Committee Against the Flag Amendment and Laws, said the group was formed when the Supreme Court decided to hear the Texas case in 1988.

Ms. Lyons identified Mr. Johnson as a member of the Revolutionary Communist Youth Brigade, which she identified as the "youth group of the Revolutionary Communist Party."

She identified Mr. Tyler as an "artist" who has "taken the name 'Dread' Scott" and stirred controversy with a work that was shown at the Art Institute of Chicago. Titled *What Is The Proper Way To Display The U.S. Flag,* the work included a U.S. flag positioned on the floor in such a way that viewers of the exhibit were forced to step on it.

Ms. Lyons identified Mr. Eichman as a member of the Coalition Opposed to Censorship in the Arts. She said Mr. Blalock was a member of a group called Vietnam Veterans Against the War/Anti-Imperialist.

The Emergency Committee to which the four flag burners belong, Ms. Lyons said, is part of Refuse and Resist, an umbrella organization that "opposes the entire agenda of right-wing attacks and repression that is coming down on this country."

The flag-burning demonstration had been scheduled for noon on the plaza of the Supreme Court, but the organizers shepherded photographers and television cameras across the street to the center steps of the Capitol's East Front, the setting for presidential inaugurations before 1981.

The demonstration began when one of the four produced a flag and ripped it to pieces, which two Capitol police officers tore from his hands. Simultaneously, a second protester produced a flag and set it afire, and two other flags were torched with lighters and matches before police took the four into custody.

As police tried to stamp out the flames, then turned fire extinguishers on them, the demonstrators chanted, "Burn, baby, burn" and "Stop the fascist flag law. Oppose it."

Mr. Nichols said crime scene investigators later examined the steps and took charred remnants of the flags for evidence.

Copyright 1989 The Dallas Morning News Company

Glossary Words, Ideas, or Movements
Actions Speak Louder than Words

ABRIDGE To reduce or diminish, when speaking of rights under the law.

ANTI-WAR DEMONSTRATIONS DURING THE VIETNAM WAR In the mid-1960s, widespread anger at the United States' involvement in the Vietnam War led to a mass movement of people—students, writers, pacifists, clergy members, and even some disillusioned Vietnam veterans—who used demonstrations, parades, and sit-ins to try to force American political leaders to end the war. Some of the most visible anti-war protesters were American university students. In February, and again in March, 1965, Students for a Democratic Society (SDS) organized marches on the Oakland army terminal, the departure point for many troops bound for Southeast Asia. On March 24, faculty members at the University of Michigan held a series of "teach-ins" that sought to educate large segments of the student population about both the moral and political foundations of U.S. involvement in Vietnam. On April 17, 1965, SDS led a non-violent protest march in Washington, D.C. that made the front page of *The New York Times.*

On October 16, 1967, 120 anti-war demonstrators were arrested after a staged sit-in at the Oakland, California draft induction center. Days later, on October 21, a massive demonstration against the war took place in Washington, D.C. when a spectrum of anti-war activists marched to the Pentagon. Leaders of the war resistance called for young men to turn in their draft cards. In November, 1969, a second march on Washington drew an estimated 500,000 participants. The anti-war movement made itself seen and heard through its size and determination and figures prominently in the history of the Vietnam era.

ATTACK ON PEARL HARBOR Early on the morning of Sunday, December 7, 1941—a day that President Franklin Roosevelt proclaimed would "live in infamy"—Japanese fighter pilots attacked the U.S. naval base at Pearl Harbor, Hawaii. This surprise attack, which Japan undertook without first declaring war, provoked the United States to end its neutral stance on World War II and join the Allies (Great Britain and the Soviet Union) against the Axis Powers of Japan, Germany, and Italy. Pearl Harbor was the worst naval disaster in U.S. history, with more than 2,000 casualties, dozens of aircraft lost, and 16 ships damaged or destroyed. Congress declared war on Japan on December 8, 1941. Japan's allies, Germany and Italy, declared war on the United States on December 11.

DRAFT CARDS Draft cards were issued to all men who had registered with the Selective Service, the government agency that provides manpower to the armed forces in cases of emergency. The need for more manpower during the Vietnam War led Congress to pass the Military Selective Service Act in 1967, which required all men between the ages of eighteen and twenty-six to register for the draft. Men were required to carry their draft cards at all times. As a result, the burning of draft cards became a symbolic act against the war.

"IMMINENT LAWLESS ACTION" The key concept of the 1969 *Brandenburg v. Ohio* decision. Under this concept, free speech can only be curtailed if it creates an immediate likelihood of violence or law breaking.

Glossary Words, Ideas, or Movements
Actions Speak Louder than Words, cont.

NON-VIOLENT DEMONSTRATIONS Non-violence is based on the theory that social change can best be brought about through the use of moral as opposed to physical force. In essence, non-violent protest attempts to combat physical and political force with peaceful, non-compliant resistance; sometimes called "passive resistance." It is typically used by minority groups faced with the power of government or some other much larger force. Non-violent protesters attempt to demonstrate, by example, a contrast between themselves—and, therefore, their cause—and the more powerful forces they oppose. They do this by initiating a situation in which their opponents will be provoked to respond unjustly, either by using actual violence against the non-violent demonstrators, or by arresting and jailing them for inordinate amounts of time. The protesters' aim is to excite the sympathy of the citizenry, who will in turn put pressure on the government to act justly by freeing protesters and taking their demands seriously.

POLITICAL PROTESTS Political protests are protests against the government or the policies of the government in power. Considered a political symbol, the U.S. flag is often used in political protests because it represents the nation and its government. In the Unites States, political protests enjoy protection under the First Amendment, but the Supreme Court has upheld regulations limiting the times, places, and manner of demonstrations that interfere with the rights of others. For example, the Court has upheld the constitutionality of political demonstrations on the grounds of a state capital while striking down demonstrations at a jailhouse, where prison security could be threatened.

PROSCRIBE To condemn, outlaw, or forbid.

"REAGONOMICS" "Reaganomics" was President Ronald Reagan's supply-side economic program that endeavored to increase overall productivity by freeing American capitalism from heavy taxes and governmental regulations. Prosperity for the upper class would then trickle down to the middle and lower classes. When recession struck in 1982, it seemed as though "Reaganomics" would be discarded as a failed program. In 1983, however, the economy rebounded, as the stock market surged and inflation remained stagnant. Americas' optimism grew, encouraged by these economic factors and lower income taxes, and the consumer market flourished, leading to sustained economic growth throughout the 1980s. However, despite these signs of prosperity, the national debt skyrocketed to more than $2 trillion by 1986. The legacy of "Reaganomics" remains mixed as a result.

REPUBLICAN NATIONAL CONVENTION OF 1984 The 1984 Republican National Convention was held from August 20–23 in Dallas, Texas. President Ronald Reagan was renominated as the Republican Party's presidential candidate. Senator Barry Goldwater made a farewell speech to the convention before retiring from the U.S. Senate. Outside the convention, the Youth International Party (commonly called "Yippies"), famous for their protests of the Vietnam War, demonstrated against the Republican Party along with a group called the "Republican War Chest Tour." As a member of the Revolutionary Communist Youth Brigade, Gregory Lee Johnson burned a U.S. flag outside the convention to protest the Reagan administration's policies.

Biographies and Organizations
Actions Speak Louder than Words

*Heinen/Collection of the Supreme
Court of the United States*

BRENNAN, WILLIAM

Portrait of William Brennan, associate justice of the U.S. Supreme Court (1956–1990). During his time on the high bench, Brennan established a reputation as a defender of individual rights. His majority decision in Texas v. Johnson (1989) is considered one of the most important free speech rulings to date.

Associate Supreme Court Justice from 1956 until 1990. Brennan was born in Newark, New Jersey, in 1906 and received a law degree from Harvard. He fought in World War II. President Eisenhower appointed Brennan to the Supreme Court in 1956. A liberal force on the Court, Brennan worked closely with Chief Justice Earl Warren on several important decisions. Brennan died in 1997.

Rather than adhering strictly to the letter of the law when considering the Constitution, Brennan considered it an evolving document that must change with the needs of the greater good. He helped to increase the latitude granted to free speech during the 1960s, narrowing the definition of libel in *New York Times Co. v. Sullivan* (1964) and participating in the full-Court opinion in *Brandenburg v. Ohio* (1969). Brennan wrote the majority opinion in the case of *Texas v. Johnson* (1989), the most controversial free speech case to date.

DALLAS MORNING NEWS

The *Dallas Morning News* is a daily newspaper that operates out of Dallas, Texas. It began operating in Dallas in 1885 as a satellite edition of the *Galveston Daily News*. At the turn of the 20th century, it had a circulation of more than 15,000. It made a reputation in the 1920s for condemning the Ku Klux Klan in Texas. In 1949, the paper opened new offices on Young Street in downtown Dallas; by then, circulation was nearly 160,000. Today, *The Dallas Morning News* is one of the nation's largest newspapers, with a circulation of around 500,000. It is owned by the Belo Corporation, a media company that owns newspapers, television stations, cable news networks, and websites.

EMERGENCY COMMITTEE AGAINST THE FLAG AMENDMENT AND LAWS

The Emergency Committee Against the Flag Amendment and Laws was an advocacy group formed in 1988 before the Supreme Court heard the case of *Texas v. Johnson*. In 1989, three of its members (including Shawn Eichman) publicly protested the Flag Protection Act of 1989 by burning three flags on the steps of the U.S. Capitol. They were joined by Gregory Lee Johnson. All four men were arrested for violating the new law. Together with the Revolutionary Communist Youth Brigade, the Emergency Committee Against the Flag Amendment and Laws protested outside the Supreme Court during the hearings on the constitutionality of the Flag Protection Act of 1989. When the act was overturned, the committee held a victory celebration in New York City and invited people to come and "Burn your favorite symbol of oppression."

Biographies and Organizations
Actions Speak Louder than Words, cont.

Bettman/Corbis

JOHNSON, GREGORY LEE

Gregory Lee Johnson's conviction for burning the American flag was overturned by the U.S. Supreme Court. This opinion was upheld the following year in United States v. Eichman *(1990) and* United States v. Haggerty *(1990).*

Gregory Lee Johnson was the defendant in the case of *Texas v. Johnson* (1989). He was the leader of a grassroots political protest group called the Republican War Chest and a member of the Revolutionary Communist Youth Brigade. Both groups demonstrated outside the Republican National Convention held in Dallas, Texas in August 1984. Protesters like Johnson were opposed to the military and nuclear weapons policies of President Ronald Reagan's administration.

At his trial, Johnson explained his reasons for burning the flag: "The American flag was burned as Ronald Reagan was being renominated as president. And a more powerful statement of symbolic speech, whether you agree with it or not, couldn't have been made at that time. It's quite a just position [juxtaposition]. We had new patriotism and no patriotism."

REAGAN, RONALD

Ronald Reagan was president of the United States from 1980 to 1988. He was born on February 6, 1911 in Tampico, Illinois. Over the course of a film career that lasted until 1964, he made more than 50 movies. In 1947, he was elected to the first of five consecutive one-year terms as president of the Screen Actors Guild. In 1966, he was elected governor of California. Building on his success in that state, he ran for president in 1980 and was elected by wide margins. He was reelected in 1984. As a conservative Republican, Reagan emphasized the desirability of economic freedom and of removing the federal government from the regulation of industry and commerce. In 1994, Reagan announced he had been diagnosed with Alzheimer's disease. He died in 2004.

Reagan was an extremely popular president, but he still had critics. During his first campaign for president, Reagan promised that, if elected, he would lower taxes, increase defense spending, and reduce the budget deficit. This economic theory became known as "Reaganomics." Its results were mixed; the balanced budget never materialized, and the national debt soared. Some also charged that his economic policies benefited the wealthy at the expense of the poor. These were some issues that generated protest at the Republican National Convention of 1984, where Reagan was nominated to run for a second term.

Biographies and Organizations
Actions Speak Louder than Words, cont.

U.S. Supreme Court

REHNQUIST, WILLIAM

Portrait of William Rehnquist, associate justice of the U.S. Supreme Court (1971–1986), and chief justice (1986–2005). Rehnquist's dissent in Texas v. Johnson *(1989) has been used as the basis for many arguments to outlaw flag burning in the years since the case was decided.*

Associate Supreme Court Justice 1972 –1986; Chief Justice 1986–2005. William Rehnquist was born in Milwaukee, Wisconsin, in 1924. He served in World War II before obtaining a law degree at Stanford University in 1952. He was appointed to the Supreme Court by Richard Nixon, and appointed to succeed Warren Burger as chief justice in 1986. Rehnquist died in 2005.

William Rehnquist was a conservative political thinker whose legal rulings reflected his views. Under his leadership, the Supreme Court imposed tighter restrictions upon access to abortion and upon death-row inmates' access to final appeals. In the case of *Texas v. Johnson*, Rehnquist authored the dissenting opinion, upholding Texas' ban on burning the American flag. However, he refused to acknowledge flag burning as a free speech issue. Rehnquist protected the defendant's right to express anti-government ideas, but denied that Johnson had the right to express himself in this specific manner. His dissent has formed the basis for consequent arguments in favor of outlawing flag desecration in this country.

REVOLUTIONARY COMMUNIST YOUTH BRIGADE

The Revolutionary Communist Youth Brigade (RCYB) is the youth group of the Revolutionary Communist Party (RCP). The RCP is a Marxist-Leninist organization founded in 1975 by former members of Students for a Democratic Society (SDS). Its leaders fled to Europe in the 1980s after a demonstration at the White House. That same decade, RCYB member Gregory Lee Johnson burned a flag at the Republican National Convention, which resulted in the *Texas v. Johnson* Supreme Court case.

STEVENS, JOHN PAUL

Portrait of John Paul Stevens, associate justice of the U.S. Supreme Court (1975–). Stevens wrote the minority dissent in United States v. Eichman *(1990), contesting the* Texas v. Johnson *(1989) decision of the previous year.*

U.S. Supreme Court

Associate Supreme Court Justice, 1975–present. John Paul Stevens was born in Chicago in 1920. After working as a Japanese code breaker during World War II, he studied law at Northwestern University. After a distinguished career as an appeals judge, he was appointed to the Supreme Court in 1975.

John Paul Stevens has made a reputation for himself as a politically neutral justice. He steers away from "activism" in legal matters, preferring to be guided by precedent rather than using radical interpretations to make law.

U.S. SUPREME COURT

The U.S. Supreme Court is the highest authority in the judicial branch. It was created by the Judiciary Act of 1789, under the provisions of the Constitution. It has jurisdiction over cases relating to the Constitution, federal laws, and treaties involving the United States. The Court consists of a chief justice and eight associate justices. Any decision requires the presence of at least six justices. Decisions are determined by a simple majority and are handed down with an opinion written by one of the justices in the majority. Justices disagreeing with the majority opinion may write dissenting opinions, and justices agreeing with the outcome but disagreeing with the logic of the majority may write concurring opinions. Supreme Court justices have made a lasting impact on American history, helping to ensure that the Constitution is adapted to changing times and circumstances.

Biographies and Organizations
Actions Speak Louder than Words, cont.

Library of Congress

WARREN, EARL

Portrait of Earl Warren, chief justice of the U.S. Supreme Court (1953-1969). The Warren Court presided over some of the most important free speech legislation of the 20th century and considerably broadened the interpretation of speech protected by the First Amendment.

Chief Justice of the Supreme Court from 1953 to 1969. Warren was born in 1891 in Los Angeles, California. He received a law degree from the University of California in 1914. Although a member of the Republican Party, Warren did not adhere strictly to Party lines. He established himself as a creative thinker, open to broad interpretations of the Constitution. Warren's judicial decisions combined a sense of moral fairness with legal precedent, making him what is popularly termed an "activist" judge. Earl Warren died in 1974.

Many cases pertaining to civil rights and individual rights were decided during his term, including the landmark *Brown v. Board of Education* (1954) that outlawed segregation and *Brandenburg v. Ohio* (1969), which changed the course of American free speech legislation. During Warren's tenure, the Court's attitude toward free speech became increasingly more lenient. In nearly every case, the Warren Court handed down rulings that preserved and even expanded the personal freedoms protected under the Constitution.

Court Cases, Amendments, and Acts
Actions Speak Louder than Words

BRANDENBURG v. OHIO (1969)

Landmark case that demonstrated the Court's turn away from *Schenck v. United States* (1919) with its relatively intolerant stance on free speech. In this case, a member of the Ku Klux Klan was filmed at a Klan rally making threatening racist statements. He was prosecuted under an Ohio anti-terrorism law. The Supreme Court overturned the conviction and pronounced Ohio's law unconstitutional. The Justices rejected the "clear and present danger" test, saying that unless words were designed to lead to direct action, they could not be prosecuted.

FIRST AMENDMENT OF THE UNITED STATES CONSTITUTION

The most cherished and cited of all constitutional amendments, the First Amendment protects freedom of religion, speech, press, peaceable assembly, and petition. Although it was originally the third of twelve proposed amendments (the first two of which were not initially ratified), there is some rightful symbolism in the fact that this important amendment now heads the Bill of Rights.

FLAG PROTECTION ACT (1968)

During the 1960s and 1970s, anti-Vietnam War protesters frequently desecrated U.S. flags or representations of the flag in order to show their outrage at America's role in the war. The most highly publicized episode, a televised incident of flag burning in Central Park in April 1967, brought renewed attention to the flag and precipitated the first federal legislation on the subject. The Flag Protection Act law, adopted in 1968, provided a penalty of up to $1,000, a year in jail, or both for anyone who "knowingly cast[s] contempt upon any flag of the United States by publicly mutilating, defacing, defiling, burning, or trampling upon it." Shortly thereafter, a number of proposals were introduced in Congress to guard voluntary flag salutes in public schools and buildings and to allow Congress to protect the flag from desecration.

Court Cases, Amendments, and Acts
Actions Speak Louder than Words, cont.

FLAG PROTECTION ACT OF 1989

The Flag Protection Act of 1989 made it a federal crime to "knowingly mutilate, deface, physically defile, burn, maintain on the floor or ground, or trample upon any flag of the United States." Supporters of the act believed that this law sidestepped the constitutional issue by making flag abuse illegal in itself, regardless of the political motive of the abuser or the reactions of those who might be offended by it. The law, they insisted, was written to punish conduct—the act of deliberately damaging a flag—rather than speech, symbolic or otherwise. This argument failed to persuade the U.S. Supreme Court, however, which ruled the Flag Protection Act of 1989 unconstitutional in the landmark case *United States v. Eichman* (1990).

FOURTEENTH AMENDMENT

Amendment passed in 1868 as a means of enforcing the legal status granted to former slaves after the Civil War. However, the Due Process Clause of the Amendment has been cited frequently in free speech cases. The Bill of Rights pertains only to the federal government's power to restrict rights. The Due Process Clause protects the same freedoms from interference by state governments. As a result, an unconstitutional state law banning free speech violates both the First *and* Fourteenth Amendments.

SCHENCK v. UNITED STATES (1919)

This Supreme Court case took shape when an American Socialist, Charles Schenck, was prosecuted for sedition under the Espionage Act of 1917. He had sent 15,000 anti-war pamphlets through the mail to potential draftees. Schenck urged the men to refuse to fight when the United States was entering World War I and preparing to send troops overseas. Although the language was fiery, the pamphlet did not advocate violent resistance. Yet the Espionage Act had criminalized actions that aided America's enemies. Anyone who tried to deprive the United States of soldiers was technically helping the enemy. By labeling protest an act of treason, the Espionage Act set an individual's right to speak freely against the nation's right to look after its own interests. The *Schenck* case was about deciding which right took precedence.

Two important concepts arose from the Supreme Court's unanimous decision in *Schenck v. United States*. As written by Justice Oliver Wendell Holmes, they are central to understanding the course of free speech legislation in the modern United States.

1. "falsely shouting fire in a theater and causing a panic": Holmes' famous and oft-quoted analogy from this opinion stated that free speech was not absolute, but rather had to be looked at within its context.

2. "clear and present danger" test: taking its cue from the "shouting fire" idea, this test dictates that freedom of speech should be restricted only in cases where such speech constitutes a clear and present danger that Congress has a right to prevent.

Court Cases, Amendments, and Acts
Actions Speak Louder than Words, cont.

TAYLOR v. MISSISSIPPI (1943)

In March, 1942, the state of Mississippi passed a law that made it a felony to speak or disseminate any teachings or printed matter designed to "encourage violence, sabotage, or disloyalty to the government of the United States, or the state of Mississippi" or to "create an attitude of stubborn refusal to salute, honor or respect the flag or government of the United States, or of the state of Mississippi." The state passed the law as a means of protecting public safety and the security of the United States while it was at war. Three individuals were found guilty of violating the law in June, 1942 and were each sentenced to one year in prison. The Supreme Court reversed the convictions in *Taylor v. Mississippi* because it found that the Mississippi law violated the First and Fourteenth amendments.

UNITED STATES CONSTITUTION

The "supreme law of the land," the U.S. Constitution was drafted by legislators in Philadelphia, Pennsylvania between July and September 1787. The delegates had originally met to revise the Articles of Confederation (the first document to frame the U.S. government), but decided instead to discard the Articles and create an entirely new form of government. The delegates worked to achieve a delicate balance by establishing a government powerful enough to be effective but not oppressive. The resulting document establishes the country's republican principles, outlines the checks and balances between the three branches of government, and suggests the federalist relationship between the national and state governments. After New Hampshire ratified the document on June 21, 1788, the new form of government had the necessary support of three-fourths of the states to go into effect, which it did on July 2 of that year. The U.S. Constitution has remained at the center of American government ever since.

UNITED STATES v. EICHMAN (1990)

United States v. Eichman was one of several cases that stemmed directly from passage of the Flag Protection Act of 1989. In this case, Shawn Eichman had burned a flag on the steps of the U.S. Capitol to protest American policies. A second case, *United States v. Haggerty* (1990), was argued at the same time. A Seattle man had burned a flag as a direct challenge to the Flag Protection Act itself. In response to both cases, Justice William Brennan cited the precedent set in *Texas v. Johnson,* and the Court struck down the Flag Protection Act.

UNITED STATES v. O'BRIEN (1968)

One of several controversial cases regarding freedom of speech in relation to the Vietnam War, *United States v. O'Brien* rejected the claims of O'Brien that burning his draft card had been a form of political expression and thus was protected under the First Amendment's guarantee of free speech. The Supreme Court also established a test by which to determine if government interests outweighed the claims of personal liberty in regards to free speech. First, the government had to show a compelling interest, and second, that interest had to be unrelated to the suppression of free speech.

Court Cases, Amendments, and Acts
Actions Speak Louder than Words, cont.

WEST VIRGINIA STATE BOARD OF EDUCATION v. BARNETTE (1943)
West Virginia State Board of Education v. Barnette arose from a policy enforced by the State Board of Education that required school children to salute the American flag. Refusal was grounds for expulsion and a charge of delinquency. The Supreme Court ruled that the policy was a violation of the First Amendment. Justice Robert Jackson wrote in the majority opinion that "no official, high or petty, can prescribe what shall be orthodox in politics, nationalism, religion, or other matters of opinion or force citizens to confess by word or act their faith therein." Even in wartime, national unity could only be encouraged; it could not be forced.

Sources

New York Times v. Sullivan, 376 US 254 (1964)

Brown v. Board of Education, 347 US 483 (1954)

Taylor v. Mississippi, 319 US 583 (1943)

Additional Resources

- Using This Resource Book

- Integration into National History Day

- Using ABC-CLIO Websites for Researching Free Speech

- Additional Free Speech Topic Ideas

Using This Resource Book

The *Triumph & Tragedy* resource books are designed to provide teachers with all the materials to create interactive lessons centered on a single important topic of American history. In each lesson, the students are asked to analyze primary historical documents and draw conclusions about the topic. You will find two sets of suggested classroom activities in each workbook. For each activity, we have provided background essays, source documents, and reference pieces.

The materials are organized as follows:

1. INTRODUCTION

The essay in this section is a broad overview of the resource book's topic. You may use it to create a general lesson or lecture on the issue at hand, or to prepare students for the historical analysis portions.

2. THROUGHOUT HISTORY

The material provided here is geared to a specific sub-topic within the broader issue; for example, the role of work in immigration or the legal aspects of free speech. This material may be used to create a preparatory lecture for the resource book's interactive portions, or copied and handed out for the students to read.

3A & 3B. DEFINING MOMENTS

Two key historical events are presented in each resource book that illustrate the problems and complex forces at work within each issue. The Defining Moment sections begin with short historical background essays that contextualize the historical event. Again, these pieces may be used to organize a short presentation or given to students to read before beginning the activities.

4A & 4B. CLASSROOM ACTIVITY

Each Defining Moment has a Classroom Activity attached. The Activity is broken down into parts, with materials required for each part of the Activity noted. When the Activity calls for Activity Sheets, these are located with the Activity description. In some cases, each portion of the Activity may stand alone, but they are designed to be cumulative. The last part draws on the lessons of the earlier parts, making it the most comprehensive. Some lessons are designed to take up a full class period, some are shorter, and some require homework assignments. The teacher will need to determine what is appropriate for his or her class based upon allotted time and teaching goals.

5A & 5B. PRIMARY SOURCES

The historical documents, images, cartoons, etc. called for in the Classroom Activities are in this section, each piece designed to be reproduced for the students. At the end of the Primary Sources are reference sources: glossary words, information on important laws, difficult quotes, background essays, etc. The teacher may wish to make handouts or overheads of this material, or write some of the information on the board to help the students with unfamiliar vocabulary or concepts.

We hope you find this format user-friendly and that you are able to adapt it easily to your students' needs.

Integration into National History Day

NHD
NATIONAL
HISTORY DAY

The theme *Triumph & Tragedy in History* is an excellent backdrop for historical research surrounding issues of freedom of speech. As the court cases were presented in this resource book, an image of individuals motivated by passionate beliefs emerged. Some were triumphant in their quest to uphold their First Amendment rights; others endured tragic circumstances because of their convictions.

The issues surrounding freedom of speech are complex, interpretative, and relevant; all excellent qualities for a National History Day research project.

National History Day engages students in historical research. After selecting a topic related to the NHD annual theme, students conduct research into primary and secondary sources. They enter their final projects in competitions using one of four different presentation formats: research paper, performance, exhibit, or documentary.

National History Day projects ask students to determine the historical significance of their chosen topics. Projects related to free speech can be approached using different research processes:

- Using primary and secondary documents to place the topic into historical perspective
- Building a timeline of events leading to the conflict to illustrate the significance of the topic
- Presenting an analysis of the conflict through the introduction of the historical context and the people involved to deepen historical understanding

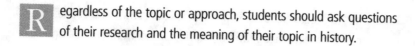

R egardless of the topic or approach, students should ask questions of their research and the meaning of their topic in history.

1. Who were the people involved?

2. What were their motivations?

3. Why did the incident occur at this time in history?

4. What was gained and what price was paid?

5. What were the long-term effects of the court case?

Happy researching!

Complete guidelines and more information can be accessed at

WWW.NHD.ORG

Using ABC-CLIO Websites for Researching Free Speech

The ABC-CLIO Schools Social Studies Subscription websites combine reference material, curriculum, current events, and primary sources in a single resource to help make historical research straightforward, accessible, and exciting for students. They provide students with the tools they need to investigate and assess the important questions associated with the topic of free speech. Questions to consider include:

What does the First Amendment to the Constitution of the United States say about freedom of speech? Under what circumstances has speech in the United States been regulated and why?

What arguments support unregulated individual expression? What arguments support the regulation of free speech?

How have attitudes toward free speech changed in the United States over time?

How have Supreme Court decisions affected the evolution of free speech regulation in the United States?

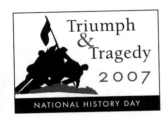

With these websites, students can find entries related to the topic of free speech that link to related reference and primary source material, providing historical context that will help students develop their skills of source evaluation and historical analysis. Teachers can construct customized research lists of reference entries, images, maps, and documents, allowing students to compare, contrast, and analyze a variety of related resources.

ABC-CLIO's social studies subscription websites:

- Provide students access to deeper and broader content than other social studies resources, allowing students to synthesize what they learn from reference material and primary sources
- Combine reference, curriculum, and current events, which are updated daily
- Are correlated to curriculum standards, key assessments, and major textbooks
- Meet the needs of students for different grade levels and assignments
- Provide access from school and home for students and faculty